## Strategies for Living Unlimited

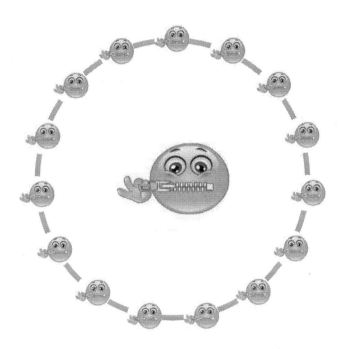

# LET'S WORK IT OUT:
# *THE POWER OF THE ZIP* WORKBOOK

By Jill Kamp Melton

# Let's Work It Out:
## *The Power of the Zip* Workbook

By Jill Kamp Melton

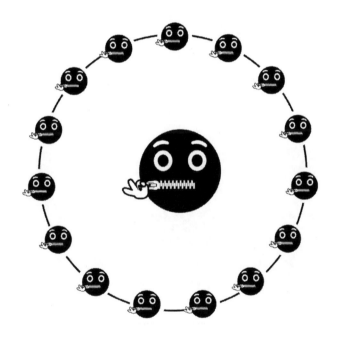

Printed in the United States of America

First Printing: 2018

ISBN-13: 978-1717178299

ISBN-10:1717178294


2500 N. Van Dorn Street, Ste. 902
Alexandria, VA 22302


www.strategiesforlivingunlimited.com

# Table of Contents

# INTRODUCTION

**The Power of the Zip** and this companion workbook give you the tools to change yourself, and also to trigger change in others.

*But, who needs to change?* All of us.

*Why?* Culture, communities, families, organizations, individuals, and all relationships are constantly evolving.

But our human nature makes us resistant to change. Fear and uncertainty can cripple us in the face of change, but the right tools, self-awareness, and inspired coaching can help us through the change process so that we can thrive.

*What is the goal of change?* These are some of the most important: maturity, healthy relationships, and the ability to grow throughout one's lifetime. The definition of personal and professional health is the ability to be "fully present in the present," and to be logical, self-aware, spiritually alive, capable of transformation, and willing to change, both personally and professionally when necessary. These traits are also present in those who have the greatest maturity.

Individuals and groups that want maturity and emotional health for themselves and their organizations view change with expectation, wonder and curiosity. They want to thrive in the midst of change, and want to inspire others to do the same.

It is up to each of us to reinvent our lives, for our own sakes and for those we live with, work with, and interact with. Coping with change is not a solo activity. **The Power of the Zip** (POZ) and this workbook help you navigate the messy dynamics of culture, communities, families, organizations, and relationships.

If we don't change, the noise of the crowd will deafen us, turning us into either combatants or recluses. If we don't embrace change, the pressures of change around us make us fearful, so that we run from others and from change. When we resist change, we miss the opportunities that we encounter everyday to learn and grow, to become more than we ever thought possible.

Remember, the reward for deciding to work toward maturity and emotional health is a life filled with expectation and wonder, in a world that is brimming with opportunities.

It is up to each of us, individually, to reinvent ourselves and our leadership, not just for our own personal gratification but to help others do the same.

Strategies for Living Unlimited is your transformational change agent, ready to help you navigate the murky waters of change for your good, for your health, for your maturity and for your relationships.

# BEFORE WE BEGIN

## Expectations

What are your expectations for using this book? List your own, then list those suggested by others.

_____

_____

_____

_____

_____

_____

_____

_____

_____

## Quote

*"Be clear about your expectations and then try to exceed them."*                    Jill Kamp Melton

## Goals for this course
(Circle those you think you need more of)

- To be fully heard and understood

- To listen more effectively

- To recalibrate my skills where necessary

- To practice relationship repair using effective listening and speaking

- To de-escalate hostility in conversations and relationships

- To eliminate confusion in conversations and relationships

- To enhance connections between people and prevent dangling/isolation

- To replace hate in relationships with hope

- To attract others instead of repelling them

- To appreciate my own uniqueness and the uniqueness of others

# How To Use This Workbook

This workbook can be used either in a classroom setting or as a personal self-directed study.

In a classroom setting, you will be guided by a facilitator to explore each concept and discuss, role play, and record your insights. Working in a group setting with others helps each member go beyond the insights and potential behavior changes he or she can come up with on his or her own.

If you are going through this workbook on your own, as a private self-examination study, we encourage you to contact us at https://www.strategiesforlivingunlimited.com/ for private coaching so that you will get the most out of the experience and what is being taught. You will experience even greater transformation if you do so.

In the "Chart and Share Lessons Learned" section in each chapter, if you are working in a classroom setting, record all the new ideas that have come to you as a result of discussion with others. If you are working on your own, keep track of your discoveries, your questions, your concerns, and your action items by writing them down. Doing this will help you grow even more in understanding.

The "Know-Feel-Act" exercise at the end of each chapter is the place where you put it all together. Know, Feel, and Act are the three pillars of the transformation process, and we urge you to incorporate them into your work.

The first step is that you have to really **know** something—the concept, the logic of it, the context for it—and how this fits in with what you already know. In many cases, it may be new to you.

The second step is that you need to **feel** connected to this concept that is new to you. Emotions are powerful. Refer to *The Power of the Zip*, Chapter 34: The Power of Emotion for a list of the many emotions you may experience but may not ever have taken time to explore. Whenever you experience a powerful emotion in the process of learning something new, go to the list and circle the words that describe what you are feeling. Doing this will result in valuable clarity for you.

The third step is that you need to **act** on what you now know and what you feel. Without intentional action, the changes you attempt will not take hold. Change is an action, not a thought or a feeling. And without action, there is no real change, and certainly no transformation.

Get ready! This journey will bring you the thrill of understanding, depths of feeling, and a transformed you.

# 1. REPAIRING RELATIONSHIPS

## Definition

A relationship that needs repair is a relationship in which one party feels unimportant, unappreciated, and not valued. That party may feel disrespected and feel he is better off without the relationship. One person may act like a bully or a victim or someone who spreads his or her own unhappiness in the relationship even though the relationship may not be the cause of happiness.

### What it is

A relationship that needs repair looks miserable or appears to be somewhat disturbed. There are so many faces of relationships that need repair. Like a home appliance, the range of damage varies, from a minor ding on the surface to a deep gash.

### What it isn't

A relationship that is not headed to the repair shop works well. The people in it interact in healthy ways and discuss small upsets as they come along so that those upsets don't fester. Healthy relationships work for those in it, and they don't complain or vent about one another.

## Assessments

The assessments in the following chapters of ***The Power of the Zip*** will help you determine if a relationship is broken.

- Chapter 2 - The Power of Perspectives, **p. 4** - *Connection Assessment*; **p. 16** - *Communication Style Self-Assessment*
- Chapter 6 - The Power of Wait, **pp. 39-41** - *Self-Assessments - Conversation*
- Chapter 8 - The Power of Listening, **p. 53** - *Assessment for Effective Listening, Assessment for Listening that Needs Improvement*
- Chapter 10 - The Power of Words, **pp. 64-66** - *How You Use Language A & B*
- Chapter 23 - The Power of Vocal Tone, **p. 122** - *Voice Improvement Assessment*
- Chapter 27 - The Power of Facial Expressions, **p. 141** - *Habits and Mannerisms to Change*
- Chapter 31 - The Power of Conversation, **p. 160** - *What is Your "Normal" Conversation?*

# Relationship Killers

Stop Engaging in These Conversational Behaviors
If You Want People in Your Life

| | | |
|---|---|---|
| Wearing the wrong hat | Abusing others with language | Giving unsolicited advice |
| Lack of discernment as to what is important to the other person | Lack of appropriate conversational etiquette and tact | Eye contact that withers, wavers, or jumps (judgmental) |
| Indulging in parallel conversations | Pretending to be open when you have a hidden agenda | Bundling many topics into one |
| Believing assumptions | Being judgmental | Avoiding with silence |
| Using vocal tone that alienates | Over-promising and under-delivering | Refusing to apologize when you are wrong |
| Using coarse language | Criticizing others | Not being present |
| Jumping in at the wrong time and/or interrupting | Talking too much | Listening to the heckler within you |
| Venting and spouting | Poor articulation | Needing to be right |
| Being blind to the fact that you are sense-of-humor challenged | Interrogating instead of questioning with curiosity | Clinging to attitudes based on preconceived ideas |
| Taking more than giving | Rarely smiling | Speaking out of desperation |
| Arguing as a habit or sport | Being emotionally unaware and/or stingy* | Lack of emotional intelligence |

*"When we deny our dark emotions, we become passive/aggressive, belligerent or even abusive." Dr. Patrick Williams[1]

Add your own:

---

[1] Master Certified Coach (International Coach Federation) and a Board Certified Coach (Center for Credentialing and Education). He has been a licensed psychologist since 1980, and began executive coaching in 1990 with Hewlett Packard, IBM, Kodak and other companies.

**Identifying relationship killers**

List the people with whom you have a relationship that needs improving.

Using the "Relationship Killers" chart on the previous page, list the behavior that applies.

| Name of Person | Relationship Killer that Applies |
|---|---|
|  |  |
|  |  |
|  |  |
|  |  |
|  |  |
|  |  |
|  |  |
|  |  |
|  |  |
|  |  |
|  |  |

**What to do to fix broken relationships**

Reframe opportunities: Instead of taking offense at what the other person has said or done, look for opportunities to find common ground.

List what those might be:

Talk about it with others: Find out what other people do when they think they are faced with a broken relationship or an impasse.

List what they do

Engage in activities that require give-and-take, sharing, and conversation. Talk about movies, books, restaurants, favorite travel destinations. Ask, "What about this topic interests you? Help me to understand your interest."

# Related Topics in POZ*

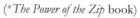
*(*The Power of the Zip book)*

Chapter 8 – The Power of Listening
Chapter 17 – The Power of the Bridge
Chapter 22 – The Power of Hospitality
Chapter 29 – The Power of the Smile
Chapter 32 – The Power of Etiquette and Tact
Chapter 36 – The Power of Expectation, Curiosity and Wonder

# Coaching

**Questions to Ask Yourself**

1. Is there anything that I say or do that might prevent me from building a relationship? List them:

    List people that this applies to:

2. How can I get information to understand how I say or do things that kill relationships and/or prevent me from building them? List assessments (including a 360 assessment):

    List people who have insight that you can trust:

## Reframe Worksheet

| What I am feeling | What I want to say | What I shouldn't say | What I should say |
|---|---|---|---|
|  |  |  |  |
|  |  |  |  |
|  |  |  |  |
|  |  |  |  |
|  |  |  |  |
|  |  |  |  |
|  |  |  |  |
|  |  |  |  |
|  |  |  |  |

## Questions to Ask Others

*Questions you can ask someone you are managing or coaching to get that person to want to change his/her behavior and build or rebuild relationships.*

1. What has worked for you in the past to repair relationships?
2. What circumstances seem to trigger a particular relationship-damaging behavior? How can you become more aware of these triggers so that you catch yourself before engaging in this behavior?
3. How can you reward yourself when you succeed in repairing a damaged relationship?
4. How can you celebrate your success?
5. If you are going to stop doing *xyz*, what positive behavior can you start doing to replace it?
6. Who would be an acceptable accountability partner for this growth step?
7. What accountability question would you like your accountability partner to ask you?

## BONUS: Questions to ask someone with whom you have a damaged relationship

1. Tell me what I can do to help me interact with you in a more effective way?
2. Do I have any habits, behaviors, words, etc. that drive you crazy and prevent us from working well together? Please let me know because I may not be aware of them.

- Conversations in relationships can sometimes turn into a sport or a fight to the finish, requiring one party to be right and the other party wrong.

- In healthy relationships, parties take turns being right and wrong. In fact, rarely is someone *TOTALLY* right or *TOTALLY* wrong.

- While people may need the validation that comes with being right, it is more helpful to reframe this mindset to: What behaviors worked, what behaviors didn't work, and what needs to be done differently.

## Activity

Role-play a difficult conversation in a difficult relationship.

Get feedback from peers on other ways this might be handled.

## Chart and Share Lessons Learned

Discuss in small groups the lessons you learned in this chapter. Write your insights on chart paper and share in small groups, then share the best insights in one large group.

```
┌─────────────┐
│   KNOW      │
│             │
│   FEEL      │
│             │
│   ACT       │
└─────────────┘
```

## Tracking Transformational Actions

What do I **know** now that I didn't know before this training?

What do I **feel** now that I was not aware of feeling before this training?

What must I **act** on to instigate change in myself, my work, and the people with whom I interact?

| Know | Feel | Act |
|------|------|-----|
|      |      |     |
|      |      |     |
|      |      |     |
|      |      |     |
|      |      |     |
|      |      |     |
|      |      |     |
|      |      |     |
|      |      |     |

## Quotes

*"I learned a lot about falling in love when I fell out of love. I learned a lot about being a friend when I was alone."*

Unknown

*"Indifference and neglect do much more damage than outright dislike."*                    J. K. Rowling

*"Forget death by lung disease. It's death by bad conversation."*
From *The Crown* (TV Show) Season 1, Episode 4 - Queen Mother tells Queen Elizabeth

# 2. CREATING A COACHING CULTURE

## Definition

A coaching culture exists in an organization when members feel free to give both positive and negative feedback to one another and to suggest ways of doing things differently. Group members know that often their conversations with each other can become coaching conversations, they look for opportunities to help each other change and they welcome being coached by one another.

### What it is

In a coaching culture, managers are mentors, skilled in helping others discover potential they may not even know they have. Both mentors and mentees ask open-ended questions, which usually begin with the words What, How or If. The atmosphere is one of openness in which all members seek to improve themselves and to help others improve as well.

The essential ingredients of a coaching culture — the vision, the mission, the initiatives, and the standards required for excellence in performance — are hammered out by teams of executives, managers and employees, all of whom have their eyes on the goal and on how to achieve it.

A coaching culture helps convert complainers into improvers, while toxic personalities who don't change may be encouraged to transition to another place of employment.

### What it isn't

A coaching culture in a professional organization is not a dictatorship where an executive defines the vision, the mission, the initiatives, and the standards required for excellence in performance.

It is not a toxic dump for complainers and malcontents.

## Assessment

Use the assessment in **_The Power of the Zip,_** Chapter 10 -The Power of Words, **pp. 64-66** -*How You Use Language - A &B*. This assessment, which you have already encountered in Chapter 1, will give you feedback as to you *how* you use language, whether effectively or recklessly. When you coach others, you need to use language with intentionality so that the person you are coaching doesn't miss your cues and become distracted by your language style.

## What's Different About a Coaching Culture?

Traditional organizations function hierarchically: with some people wielding power over others without power. "Silos" tend to develop: these are pockets of workers in vertical organizational cliques who hang together and don't interact effectively with those in other silos. Silos compete for power and resources: funds, people, space, influence, and material. New recruits wait a long time to be accepted by the people at the top of the silo, and sometimes never get it. Feedback usually contains judgmental remarks, orders, and comments that imply "My way or the highway."

When an organization of silos is transformed into one with a coaching culture, employee engagement improves, which in turn means they do better work and are more motivated to fulfill the organization's mission. Removing the "I'm the boss and you are not" mentality benefits everyone. When leaders and employees feel welcome to give one another coaching feedback, humility, the resulting vulnerability and respect for one another begins to make the workplace more hospitable for all.

Without a coaching culture, the "old boy" network rules and many workers feel that their work lives are spent in a toxic atmosphere. One employee whose boss continually berated him said he would sing in his head every song that he knew until the toxic noise of his boss' harangues stopped.

A coaching culture helps end the toxicity of bosses who bark orders and expect blind compliance. Of course, in a crisis, a leader does not stop to negotiate with others to obey. The right response in a crisis is to do what is required and not question the leader.

This is why the coaching question "What would it take to return to compliance?" is so innovative. It is not a command; it is not abusive; it is not judgmental. This question puts the responsibility of compliance on the shoulders of the employees without being mean about it.

## <u>Related Topics in POZ</u>*
*(*The Power of the Zip* book)*
(The order in which these chapters are listed is intentional.)
Chapter 9 – The Power of the Question
Chapter 8 – The Power of Listening
Chapter 5 – The Power of Silence
Chapter 6 – The Power of Wait
Chapter 7 – The Power of Pause

## <u>Coaching</u>

**Questions to Ask Yourself**

1. What do I need to know and do in order to remove my blind spots?

2. As a team member, how can I know when it is appropriate to help others on the team?

### Reframe Worksheet

| What I am feeling | What I want to say | What I shouldn't say | What I should say |
|---|---|---|---|
|  |  |  |  |
|  |  |  |  |
|  |  |  |  |
|  |  |  |  |
|  |  |  |  |
|  |  |  |  |
|  |  |  |  |
|  |  |  |  |
|  |  |  |  |

**Questions to Ask Others**

*Questions you can ask someone you are managing or coaching to get that person to want participate in building a coaching culture.*

1. What do you mean by that?
2. What would it take to return to compliance?
3. How can I support you in this project?
4. If you could do this over again, what would you do differently?

---

**<u>Key Questions to Consider</u>**
*What would it take for me to be curious enough to create a coaching culture?*
*Am I willing to do that?*

---

- Remember to ask for an invitation to coach someone. "Do you have a minute?" is a good beginning.
- Be willing to reschedule your coaching conversation if right now is not a good time.
- Coach only when it will add real value. Resist coaching if you feel lonely and just need to talk with someone.

## <u>Activity</u>

At your table group, select a project or program that is part of your work responsibilities and discuss it. Discuss bottlenecks that have occurred.

Brainstorm coaching questions to ask one another and discuss them. Practice asking these questions with the appropriate vocal tone and interest. Give feedback to one another

**Job Aid: Types of Questions and How to Use Them**

Use this Job Aid (on p. 94) when working with others to help you use questions appropriately. (You can take a photo of it on an electronic device that you carry with you.) It can coach you as you coach others. The right question asked at the right time in the right way can trigger real change.

## Lessons Learned: Chart Them and Share

Discuss in small groups the lessons you learned in this chapter. Write your insights on chart paper and share in small groups, then share the best insights in one large group.

KNOW

FEEL

ACT

## Tracking Transformational Actions

What do I **know** now that I didn't know before this training?

What do I **feel** now that I was not aware of feeling before this training?

What must I **act** on to instigate change in myself, my work, and the people with whom I interact?

| Know | Feel | Act |
|------|------|-----|
|      |      |     |
|      |      |     |
|      |      |     |
|      |      |     |
|      |      |     |
|      |      |     |
|      |      |     |
|      |      |     |
|      |      |     |

# **Quotes**

*"A coach is someone who tells you what you don't want to hear, who has you see what you don't want to see, so you can be who you always knew you could be"*

Tom Landry

*"All coaching is, is taking a player where he can't take himself."*

Bill McCartney

*"Probably my best quality as a coach is that I ask a lot of challenging questions and let the person come up with the answer."*

Phil Dixon

# 3. CULTIVATING SELF AWARENESS

## Definition

Self-awareness is a conscious knowledge of one's own character, feelings, motives, desires, and individuality. People who possess self-awareness feel comfortable in their own skin. They behave in ways that are true to themselves. Pleasing others and worrying about what other people think doesn't govern their actions.

### What it is

Self-aware people exude confidence, a sense of ease with themselves, and a thoughtful presence. They can be honest about their thoughts and feelings when interacting with others, and they give those around them a good feeling because they like themselves and are comfortable with themselves.

### What it isn't

People with little self-awareness radiate nervous insecurity and frequently seek validation from others. They are reluctant to give opinions because they think they might be wrong. They cling to people who are confident in the hope that it might rub off.

## Assessment

Access the free online assessment at: https://www.ihhp.com/free-eq-quiz/ to find out your level of Emotional Intelligence. Or contact www.talentsmart.com to take the full assessment. Read the Job Aid on p. 89.

Emotional Intelligence (EI) refers to self-awareness, self-management, social awareness, and relationship management. If your EI is not well-developed, your personal and professional relationships and work suffer. That's why self-awareness as so vital. Cultivate it and your work and relationships thrive. Ignore it and your work and your personal life deteriorate.

Blind spots in our self-awareness are common. Accepting them as permanent cripples our growth. Blind spots in self-awareness don't have to be permanent.

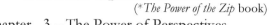

# Related Topics in POZ*

*(*The Power of the Zip book)*

Chapter   3 – The Power of Perspectives

Chapter   8 – The Power of Listening

Chapter 14 – The Power of Truth

Chapter 19 – The Power of "Taking In"

Chapter 34 – The Power of Emotion

Chapter 36 – The Power of Expectation, Curiosity and Wonder

# Coaching

**Questions to Ask Yourself**

1. Is there anything that I say or do that might prevent me from enhancing my self-awareness? List them.

2. Where can I obtain information to better understand how I say or do things that create self - awareness and/or prevent me from demonstrating those abilities (feelings, motives and desires)? List them.

3. Who are the people whose insight I can trust? List them:

## Reframe Worksheet

| What I am feeling | What I want to say | What I shouldn't say | What I should say |
|---|---|---|---|
| | | | |
| | | | |
| | | | |
| | | | |
| | | | |
| | | | |
| | | | |
| | | | |
| | | | |

## Questions to Ask Others

*Questions you can ask someone you are managing or coaching to help that person become more self-aware.*

1. What has worked for you in the past?
2. What circumstances seem to set this behavior off? How could you become more aware of these triggers so that you catch yourself before acting on these emotions?
3. What is something you could reward yourself with when you succeed in being aware of your feelings, motives, and desires and in demonstrating them in a positive manner?
4. Who would be an acceptable accountability partner for this growth step?
5. What accountability question would you like your accountability partner to ask you?

## Lessons Learned: Chart Them and Share

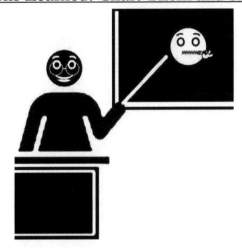

Discuss in small groups the lessons you learned in this chapter. Write your insights on chart paper and share in small groups, then share the best insights in one large group.

- Helping others figure out their unique abilities also helps you clarify your own abilities.
- In an organization, helping people understand how their abilities fit into the mission helps the mission, the individual and the team.

## Activity

This activity will create self-awareness of your unique ability. Read ***The Power of the Zip*** Chapter 21 – The Power of Discernment. **Circles of Ability**: Record your best guess of your I, C, E, and U. After discussing with others, both in this course and outside of it, review your answers and make any adjustments necessary.

**My Circles of Ability**

My I is:

_____

My C is:

_____

My E is:

_____

My U is:

_____


Regardless of how you assess your current employment and regardless of whether you are in your I, C, E, or U right now, describe the following:

- A time I was employed in my U and the impact it had on me and others

_____

- A time I was employed in my E and the impact it had on me and others

_____

- A time when I was employed in my C and the impact it had on me and others

_____

- A time when I was employed in my U and the impact it had on me and others

_____

## KNOW FEEL ACT

### Tracking Transformational Actions

What do I **know** now that I didn't know before this training?

What do I **feel** now that I was not aware of feeling before this training?

What must I **act** on to instigate change in myself, my work, and the people with whom I interact?

| Know | Feel | Act |
|------|------|-----|
|      |      |     |
|      |      |     |
|      |      |     |
|      |      |     |
|      |      |     |
|      |      |     |
|      |      |     |
|      |      |     |
|      |      |     |

## Quotes

*"If you plan on being anything less than you are capable of being, you will probably be unhappy for the rest of your life."*
Abraham Maslow

*"If you don't like something, change it. If you can't change it, change your attitude about it."*
Maya Angelou

*"Why do you sign your name a thousand times? I'm looking for the one that is me."*
from *The Chalk Garden* by Enid Bagnold

# 4. LISTENING EFFECTIVELY

## Definition

 To listen effectively means hearing, sensing, and discerning what is being said and how it is being said, and being aware of how you think and feel about what is being said. It requires being totally in the present so that you don't filter what you hear. You are a sponge absorbing all you hear so that you can repeat the essence of it without distortion.

### What it is

Listening behaviors vary because we are all different. Some people listen best while maintaining eye contact with the speaker, with few mannerisms or facial expressions that might register impatience, disagreement, or agreement with the speaker.

Others listen best while taking notes because auditory clarity is not their strength. They are visual and have to see the words in order to fully "hear" them.

Others are fidgety because they listen best by doing. A good listener may not sit still like a statue.

Speakers need to refrain from making assumptions about how well their listeners are listening. The proof of effective listening is revealed by what listeners say and do when the speaker is done. Don't think that just because the other person can't see you, because you are talking on the phone, for instance, that he or she can't detect that you are distracted because you are multitasking. Your vocal tone gives you away.

### What it isn't

Effective listening usually doesn't happen while multitasking. No matter how strenuously listeners claim they can listen fully while changing the oil in a car, preparing dinner, vacuuming, etc., multitasking is a myth that has been exposed by science. If we are to listen effectively, taking in all that is being said — including the emotion, the thoughts, what is unsaid, and the body language — we have to be fully present in the present.

## Assessment

This assessment is a coaching question you should answer in the space below:

**What do I do when I am supposed to be listening?**

Holding yourself accountable for your helpful and/or distracting listening behaviors will improve your attentiveness to the here and now.

## Related Topics in POZ\*

*(\*The Power of the Zip book)*

Chapter 3 – The Power of Caring
Chapter 4 – The Power of the Present
Chapter 5 – The Power of Silence
Chapter 6 – The Power of Wait
Chapter 7 – The Power of Pause
Chapter 8 – The Power of Listening

## Coaching

**Questions to Ask Yourself**

1.  What type of role model am I when it comes to effective listening?

2.  What behaviors should I consider adjusting when I'm listening?

3. Who do I know who holds the attention of people they speak with? Why do people hang on to every word? Why do they take notes? What factors contribute to this person's ability to enable others to listen effectively?

## Reframe Worksheet

| What I am feeling when listening | What I want to do when listening | What I shouldn't do while listening | What I should do while listening |
|---|---|---|---|
| | | | |
| | | | |
| | | | |
| | | | |
| | | | |
| | | | |
| | | | |
| | | | |
| | | | |

### Questions to Ask Others

1. What behaviors would you like to see and hear when I am listening to you?
2. What behaviors in your listeners bother you and distract you from your message when you are speaking?

### BONUS: The Power of "Gription"

When you speak with others, you do one of three things:
1. Talk about new information.
2. Talk about old information.
3. Put a new spin on old information.

The new information and the new spin on old information have the potential to hold your audience in rapt attention. News is what people crave, something new to think about, chew on, digest, and share.

When we present our ideas in a new way or present totally new ideas, it makes them easier for our listeners to remember them. This gives our presentation "gription," that is, the ability to stick in the listener's mind. What can you do to increase the "gription" of your words so that others can listen more effectively? See *The Power of the Zip*, Chapter 30 – The Power of Connection for specific phrases that enhance "gription."

- Remember to check in with your listener(s) to see if they are listening. After every sixth sentence or so, ask "What do you think about what I've been sharing?"
- Yawning and fidgeting may not always mean that your listener is not paying attention.
- Tell your listener(s) that it's okay to take notes if doing so would help them listen more effectively.

## Activity

Using the Job Aid "Steps to Active Listening" at the back of the book, select two topics to discuss with a partner. One of you opens a 2-3 minute conversation about one of the topics. The other person, the listener, responds using the "13 Steps to Better Active Listening." in the same Job Aid After 2-3 minutes, switch roles and hold a conversation on the second topic.

After each of you has had a chance to speak and to listen, discuss the pitfalls and opportunities inherent in listening.

## Lessons Learned: Chart Them and Share

Discuss in small groups the lessons you learned in this chapter. Write your insights on chart paper and share in small groups, then share the best insights in one large group.

## Tracking Transformational Actions

```
┌─────────────┐
│  KNOW       │
│             │
│  FEEL       │
│             │
│  ACT        │
└─────────────┘
```

What do I **know** now that I didn't know before this training?

What do I **feel** now that I was not aware of feeling before this training?

What must I **act** on to instigate change in myself, my work, and the people with whom I interact?

| Know | Feel | Act |
|------|------|-----|
|      |      |     |
|      |      |     |
|      |      |     |
|      |      |     |
|      |      |     |
|      |      |     |
|      |      |     |
|      |      |     |
|      |      |     |

## Quotes

*"Just because you said something doesn't mean it was heard."*  Jill Kamp Melton

*"Drawing on my fine command of the English language, I said nothing."*  Robert Benchley

*"When you talk, you are only repeating what you already know. But if you listen, you may learn something new."*
J. P. McEvoy

*"It's okay to be honest about not knowing rather than spreading falsehood. While it is often said that honesty is the best policy, silence is the second-best policy."*
Criss Jami, Killosophy

# 5. ASKING THE PERFECT QUESTION

## Definition

A question is a sentence that encourages a person to disclose information, ideas, feelings, or events that may hitherto not have been known. The perfect question is an open question, and open questions usually begins with What, How or If.

Dictionaries define "question" using words such as: interrogation, cross-examine, doubt and dispute. These words reflect the negative connotation associated with the act of questioning. These words describe what perfect questions are not.

### What it is

An open face and posture project curiosity when asking a question: you raise your eyebrows at least once, and you have a relaxed demeanor and friendly manner. Admittedly, sometimes our body language sends a different message. So, when asking an open question with curiosity, be self-aware, to ensure that there is no discrepancy in what you are trying to convey, your facial expression, and your body language.

### What it isn't

When a person asks a question with a wrinkled forehead, head tilted to one side, arms crossed in front of the chest, legs crossed tightly, and a tense rigid appearance, in all likelihood he is interrogating someone, not asking a question with curiosity. When a questioner appears closed and judgmental, the person being questioned gets nervous and begins to resist the intrusion into his or her mind. The questioner is seen as being on the offensive and this triggers a defensive response. A conflict has been started, even if that was never the intention of the questioning.

## Assessment

Pick a partner and role-play a Q & A exchange for about 2 minutes on a topic that is important to both of you. After two minutes, do a post-event assessment by asking each other these questions:

1. How would you like me to behave when questioning you?
2. What could I have done or said to appear more friendly?
3. What did I do or say that worked well?

# The Importance of Open Questions

Leaders need to use open questions as much as possible. When done successfully, you find out information, ideas, and feelings that you did not previously know.

When you ask the right question, you create the possibility of inspiring deep thought in the other person. It also gives the person time and space to consider how to answer in a way he or she might not have thought of before. Curiosity that conveys genuine interest is the mojo, the magic, the power, the charisma, and the key to opening the doors of another person's mind, heart and soul.

| Question + curiosity = ???? |
| --- |

When done poorly, you create fear, suspicion, and lack of trust.

| Question + what is already known = interrogation |
| --- |

If you ask open questions and do not find out what you did not know, you have done it badly and you need to get coaching to improve your ability to ask the perfect question.

## Related Topics in POZ*

*(*The Power of the Zip book)*

Chapter 9: The Power of Questions

**Other Resources**

See the: Job Aid on p. 94, "Types of Questions and How to Use Them."

## Coaching

**Questions to Ask Yourself**

1. When I think it's time to ask questions, what are my motives?

2. How can I recognize if I have a hidden agenda?

3. Who can I role play the Q & A with before I actually do it?

### Reframe Worksheet

| What I am feeling | What I want to say | What I shouldn't say | What I should say |
|---|---|---|---|
|  |  |  |  |
|  |  |  |  |
|  |  |  |  |
|  |  |  |  |
|  |  |  |  |
|  |  |  |  |
|  |  |  |  |
|  |  |  |  |
|  |  |  |  |

### Questions to Ask Others

1. If you could change anything about me when I ask questions, what would it be?
2. What warnings can you give me with regard to asking open questions? Please be specific.
3. What have you learned from your successes and failures?

- Questions can open doors or close doors. Intentionally chose which door you want to go through.
- Interrogation questions put people on the defensive and are generally regarded as intrusive.
- If you don't find out information or feelings or ideas after your questioning conversations, you haven't done it correctly.

**BONUS: Questions guaranteed to improve your relationships with others**

- Help me to understand. How do I begin?
- What do you want?
- How will you know when you get it?
- What do you mean by that?

The following questions, which you have already seen in an earlier chapter, are powerful questions that can be used in many different situations. If you are managing others, these questions give you leverage without being overbearing. Remember to use a benign vocal tone for greatest effect.

- What would it take to return to compliance?
- What can we do to make compliance a habit?
- How can I support you in this project?
- If you could do this over again, what would you do differently?

## **Activity**

One person thinks of something he or she has done that the rest of the group likely doesn't know about. Using the Job Aid on p. 94 *"Types of Questions and How to Use Them"* as a guide, the rest of the group asks questions to guess what it is.

Which types of questions got you closer to the answer?

Repeat this activity until several people have had a chance to field questions.

## Lessons Learned: Chart Them and Share

Discuss in small groups the lessons you learned in this chapter. Write your insights on chart paper and share in small groups, then share the best insights in one large group.

## Tracking Transformational Actions

**KNOW**

**FEEL**

**ACT**

What do I **know** now that I didn't know before this training?

What do I **feel** now that I was not aware of feeling before this training?

What must I **act** on to instigate change in myself, my work, and the people with whom I interact?

| Know | Feel | Act |
|------|------|-----|
|      |      |     |
|      |      |     |
|      |      |     |
|      |      |     |
|      |      |     |
|      |      |     |
|      |      |     |
|      |      |     |
|      |      |     |

# Quotes

*"The best scientists and explorers have the attributes of kids! They ask questions and have a sense of wonder. They have curiosity. 'Who, what, where, why, when and how!' They never stop asking questions, and I never stop asking questions, just like a five year old."*

Sylvia Earle

*"If you do not know how to ask the right question, you discover nothing."*

W. Edwards Deming

# 6. GIVING EFFECTIVE FEEDBACK

## Definition

Feedback used to refer to the sound distortion created by a malfunctioning microphone or amplifier. But today, the word is more commonly used to describe specific reactions to a product or a person's performance, usually for the purposes of improvement. So, what used to be a word referring to an annoying sound is now used as welcoming words of encouragement and instruction. In this workbook, the definition of feedback is, "**What you saw and what you heard, and the impact that it had.**"

Without feedback, we are unaware of the impact — be it positive or negative — we have on others, and that can negatively impact our ability to change or improve. With feedback, we become aware of our blind spots and our successes, which enables us to improve and to become more mature and professional in our work lives and mature in our personal lives.

Details on how to give feedback and how to receive it are provided in the Job Aid on p. 92, "How to Give and Receive Feedback." Refer to it when doing the Activity for this chapter.

| What it is | What it isn't |
| --- | --- |
| An effective feedback conversation exhibits little angst and lots of trust. Positive body language and word choice, silence, and civility are the hallmarks of this conversation. | Feedback is not mean spirited negative criticism. It is not a vehicle for arguments, sniping, being defensive, or slinging insults and judgments at each another. When feedback is not given effectively, anger, immaturity, self-centeredness and lots of drama are on display. |

## Assessments

You have used these assessments before. Use them again to help uncover blind spots that get in the way of providing feedback effectively: ***The Power of the Zip,*** Chapter 10 - The Power of Words, **p. 64-66** *How You Use Language A & B*

## Related Topics in POZ*

(*The Power of the Zip book)

## Coaching

**Questions to Ask Yourself**

1.  Do I have a hidden agenda with this person? If so, what is it?

2.  Is there anything I want to say to this person that is immature and/ or unprofessional?

3.  Am I tempted to want to "fix" this person?

---

### *What can you do with feedback?*

**You can use it.**

**You can lose it.**

**You can store it and revisit it later.**

---

### Reframe Worksheet

| What I am feeling | What I want to say | What I shouldn't say | What I should say |
|---|---|---|---|
| | | | |
| | | | |
| | | | |
| | | | |
| | | | |
| | | | |
| | | | |
| | | | |
| | | | |

## Questions to Ask Others

1. How do you handle feedback when you don't like the person to whom you are giving it?
2. What pitfalls can you warn me about when I have to give feedback to someone I do not respect or like?
3. If I am tempted to be critical, what words can I use to soften my message and to encourage the other person?

---

### Key Question to Consider
*What is the purpose of feedback?*

---

- Feedback mirrors another person's behavior back to them.
- Feedback is not coaching.
- Feedback is neutral without judgment; coaching requires some judgment and opinion.

## Activity

Choose one person to give feedback to about something he or she has done or said in the course of this training. Follow the protocols listed in the Job Aid on p. 92, "How to Give and Receive Feedback." When you are done, the other person responds. When the other person is done, continue and also critique the feedback you just received.

Take turns until everyone has had a chance giving *and* receiving feedback.

## Lessons Learned: Chart Them and Share

Discuss in small groups the lessons you learned in this chapter. Write your insights on chart paper and share in small groups, then share the best insights in one large group.

<table>
<tr><td>KNOW</td></tr>
<tr><td>FEEL</td></tr>
<tr><td>ACT</td></tr>
</table>

## Tracking Transformational Actions

What do I **know** now that I didn't know before this training?

What do I **feel** now that I was not aware of feeling before this training?

What must I **act** on to instigate change in myself, my work, and the people with whom I interact?

| Know | Feel | Act |
|------|------|-----|
|      |      |     |
|      |      |     |
|      |      |     |
|      |      |     |
|      |      |     |
|      |      |     |
|      |      |     |
|      |      |     |
|      |      |     |

# Quotes

*"Feedback is a gift. If it doesn't feel like a gift, it's not feedback."*                    AnnMarie Valenti

*"If you can't think of anything nice to say, you're not thinking hard enough."*      Kid President (Robby Novak), an inspirational speaker on YouTube who delivered a TED Talk in 2013 at the age of 9.

*"Make feedback normal. Not a performance review."*                    Ed Batista

# 7. BUILDING TEAMS

## Definition

In a work environment, team building is the process by which those in a group interact with one another to increase healthy productive relationships with bosses, peers and employees; to enhance problem solving, decision making, role clarification and goal setting; and to improve role assignments and descriptions of tasks.

### What it is

Whether in leadership courses, management resources, job aids, and social media blogs, all these educational sources emphatically agree: Team building is the most important investment an agency can make for the workforce. Its benefits: include building trust, mitigating conflict, encouraging communication, and increasing collaboration, to name just a few. These benefits in turn raise employee engagement. Who among us doesn't want to be engaged? It is a basic human need to "feel" wanted and valued.

Consider how successful the group outcomes would be if you focused on encouraging team members to work together to meet the project goals and objectives. Facilitating a meeting of colleagues who have the potential to contribute creativity, a wide range of abilities, experience, knowledge, and strengths can inspire you to spur them to contribute even more by showing them the value of the mission and the project. At the same time think about all of the value you add to a team and what could spur you to add more.

### What it isn't

A team is unhealthy when team members talk over one another or when no one minds that some team members are ignored. A group of brilliant and excellent workers who all work independently may be productive but they are not a team. Teams should not be leaderless, aimless, disrespectful of one another, mean, or have no trust for one another.

# Assessment

The best team building assessment experiences are activities that require 100% participation. Such activities are important to discover where the bottlenecks are; e.g. emotions, distractions, assumptions, culture, or communication difficulties. They help the team to let go of ineffective mental models and adopt new ones, employ more inclusive and flexible methods to get tasks done, and to communicate about these new models more effectively.

This is an interactive assessment exercise. If you are using this workbook on your own, you will need to gather several friends to experiment with.

Begin by creating some kind of activity where you must move objects from place to place, perhaps in piles or in buckets, on the floor or on tables. Make sure there is a start and a finish. Time the group as it works on the activity.

Then do it a second time to try to shave time off the first attempt takes 6 minutes BUT without discussing how to improve the process. That is, try to nonverbally communicate how to redo the activity faster.

Observe everyone's behavior: who were the active participants, who were the watchers, and who didn't engage at all? What does your own participation tell you about how you function in a team? What did others discover about their own inclinations on a team project?

Your answers will detail with surprising accuracy how you work in a team and what team dynamics make or break team work.

In addition, be aware that working with people who are different from you can affect the health of a team. So, when a team is comprised of people of different ages, races, and/or appearances, and/or who have different abilities or values, it is vital that the team-building exercise is devised in such a way that everyone participates and that everyone's input is valued.

## <u>Coaching</u>

**Questions to Ask Yourself**

1. When I work in a team, do I cooperate, want to take over, or withdraw and let others do the heavy lifting?

2. How can I overcome my tendency to take over?

3. How can I overcome my tendency to withdraw?

4. How can I cooperate more fully?

### Reframe Worksheet

| What I am feeling | What I want to say | What I shouldn't say | What I should say |
|---|---|---|---|
| | | | |
| | | | |
| | | | |
| | | | |
| | | | |
| | | | |
| | | | |
| | | | |
| | | | |

### Questions to Ask Others

1. What problems do you see in our team that we need to address before trying to accomplish our tasks? Use the SWOT acronym (Strengths, Weaknesses, Opportunities, Threats) to help you answer this question.
2. What strengths do you see in our team?
3. What weaknesses or bottlenecks do we need to overcome?
4. What opportunities do we have that we have not leveraged?
5. What threats do you see that might affect the ability of our team to accomplish our mission?

---

### Key Question to Consider
*What is the vision without which our team has no reason to exist?*

---

- All team members need to know the vision for their work. Without it, some individuals may go rogue, resulting in many separate teams, not one focused team.
- When team work seems to fade, have a meeting to refocus on the vision. You may discover that there has been no unanimity of thought about it.

## Activity

Divide everyone into small groups to do a "Strengths, Weaknesses, Opportunities, Threats" (SWOT) analysis using the questions in "Questions to Ask Others" above.

Follow up with a vision-casting activity. Have everyone contribute to setting the team's future direction, adding something inspiring to the vision, outlining the potential for innovation in accomplishing the vision, or identifying a case study that can make the vision real.

## Lessons Learned: Chart Them and Share

Discuss in small groups the lessons you learned in this chapter. Write your insights on chart paper and share in small groups, then share the best insights in one large group.

| KNOW |
| :---: |
| FEEL |
| ACT |

## Tracking Transformational Actions

What do I **know** now that I didn't know before this training?

What do I **feel** now that I was not aware of feeling before this training?

What must I **act** on to instigate change in myself, my work, and the people with whom I interact?

| Know | Feel | Act |
|---|---|---|
|  |  |  |
|  |  |  |
|  |  |  |
|  |  |  |
|  |  |  |
|  |  |  |
|  |  |  |
|  |  |  |
|  |  |  |

## Quotes

*"Community is messy."*                                    Heather Zempel

*"Teamwork is the fuel that allows common people to attain uncommon results."*                    Andrew Carnegie

# 8. HANDLING HOT TOPICS

## Definition

A hot topic is one that makes you uncomfortable or makes your blood boil.

Arguments, which are exchanges of diverging or opposite views, often become heated or angry when they are about hot topics. Clashes over hot topics are also called quarrels, disagreements, squabbles, fights, clashes or altercations.

A discussion about a hot topic can be reasonable if the speaker uses logic, critical thinking, and open questions.

The best outcome of a hot topic conversation is the de-escalation of potential violence and the introduction of understanding. The discovery of even the smallest bit of common ground by those in the conversation has the potential to cool tempers, which in turn means there is a chance for respect to grow rather than antipathy and judgment.

### What it is

Professional, reasoned conversation about a hot topic is calm and measured. Civility governs the exchange, and if the people conversing have a serious difference of opinion, these are handled firmly and with passion as well as respect.

### What it isn't

A conversation about a hot topic that is professional and reasoned is not loud, chaotic, or abusive. It is not a chance to vent, whine, complain, and yell. It is not an argument. It does not end with a winner and a loser, or sometimes with two losers.

A hot topic conversation run amok is emotional and unpleasant. At least one participant wishes he or she had never gotten into the conversation in the first place.

# How to Handle a Conversation about a Hot Topic

**Be emotionally aware**

Preparation is vital for a successful conversation about a hot topic. Using the "Checklist of Emotions" on pp. 180-182 in *__The Power of the Zip__*, do an inventory of your emotions. Be clear as to what you are feeling and understand why it is important to resist spraying your feelings into the conversation. If your emotions are intense, you may need to role-play this conversation several times in order to master your emotions.[2]

These tips will help you begin a "hot topic" discussion:

1. Say, "You seem to have lots of ideas about (the hot topic). Help me understand your point of view."
2. Listen patiently and do not mentally rehearse your response. **Stay curious.**
3. When the other person is finished, thank him or her for taking the time to walk you through his or her ideas. Before you say anything else, consider how you feel. Consider what you think. Consider what you want to say. Then consider what you *should* say. For instance, "Thank you for sharing so freely. I appreciate your views and I would like to take some time to think about them. In the meantime, help me understand more about what you are saying."
4. "I have more questions than answers. When you say, *xxx*, what do you mean by that?" Repeat that as often as necessary. **Stay curious.**
5. Continue to affirm the emotions and the other person's concerns. When appropriate, say, "We seem to agree on *xxx*. What I'm not sure about is *xyz*. What else can you tell me? What do you recommend I read to learn more about your positions? Thank you for all of this. You've given me a lot to think about." **Stay curious.**

**Don't take or give offense**

When we take offense because of something someone has said or done to us, we are behaving as though the other person wanted to hurt us and we respond by behaving in a hurt manner. Most of the time, others don't want to hurt us. They lash out because they are angry or feeling hurt themselves and they cannot handle their feelings. It's easier to dump them on someone else, and you are simply the nearest target.

Even if they meant to hurt you, you don't have to engage in a hurting contest. You can detach and get out of the way.

---

[2] FBI hostage negotiators help hostage takers label their feelings so the hostage takers can de-escalate their emotions. See: www.theladders.com

Detachment in the midst of a potentially violent interaction is how you save yourself and the other person from further violence and damage. When we intentionally detach, we are choosing to pause and reflect on what has happened and on how we can de-escalate the moment. We choose to pour water on ourselves and the other person instead of pouring oil on a flame.

Detachment doesn't produce the adrenaline rush that a fight triggers. Detachment is a mature choice and requires self-control for success. Practice it so that you can detach before you and others hurt each other.

**Be aware that personality disorders can distort conversations about hot topics**

Be aware of at least these four types of people:

- Those who are unable to recognize that they are wrong.
- Narcissists who believe the world according to them is the only way.
- Those who are so humble that they let those who can't admit they are wrong, have their way.
- Those who kindly and lovingly let narcissists speak without ever giving them feedback.

Many times, feedback given to these types of people is simply not heard.

What is the remedy?

Sometimes it is necessary to agree to disagree. Sometimes it is necessary to take a break, a time out, until tempers cool. Sometimes it is necessary to stop engaging significantly with this person. Even if you have to fire someone who works for you, you can still do it respectfully, helping him or her figure out a better place to work.

**BONUS #1: Tips**
- Refuse to raise your voice and argue. Ask clarifying questions. Continuously look for common ground. Don't say the word "BUT." Validate what was said, then reply with, "I would like to know more."
- If you become weary, ask for a break. Say, "This conversation is challenging, deep, and worth having. I just need more time to ponder."
- Take the time out. Be firm about not getting drawn back into the discussion and do not take offense. Hot topics are not about you; they are about others, and about issues and preferences. Give up the need to be right. **Stay curious.**

## Assessments

Go through the "7 Ways to Find Out if You Are a Bully" in **The Power of the Zip**, pp. **176-177**. Circle any of the seven characteristics that might be true for you. Because we are all human, at least one will be true for you sometimes. If you disagree, research blind spots.

Also take the assessment to discover your "normal conversation" in **The Power of the Zip** - Chapter 31 - The Power of Conversation, **p. 160**.

## Related Topics in POZ*

(*The Power of the Zip book)

Chapter 31 – The Power of Conversation
Chapter 34 – The Power of Emotion
Chapter 13 – The Power of Unbundling

## Coaching

**Questions to Ask Yourself**

1. What triggers my bad behavior when I get hot about a hot topic?

2. What can I do to detach before I attack?

## Reframe Worksheet

| What I am feeling | What I want to say | What I shouldn't say | What I should say |
|---|---|---|---|
| | | | |
| | | | |
| | | | |
| | | | |
| | | | |
| | | | |
| | | | |
| | | | |
| | | | |

## Questions to Ask Others

1. What triggers your emotions when one of your hot topics comes up in conversation?
2. What makes you feel that you must contribute?
3. If you are going to wait before jumping into a hot topic conversation, how can you manage your emotions while you wait?
4. What language styles do you use when talking about a hot topic?
5. How can you intentionally change your approach to your hot topic conversational style?
6. What kind of feedback would you like that would help you cope with hot topic conversations?

---

### Key Question to Consider
*What gets in the way of you listening in an open way*
*when a hot topic is being discussed?*

---

- Depth of feeling is not wrong in a hot topic conversation as long as your intellect stays clear and focused.
- Repeatedly find common ground when opinions differ. Don't tire of this. Common ground anchors all parties in a conversation about a hot topic.

## Bonus #2: How to win an argument

1. First, reframe the situation. This is not a competition. It is an opportunity to build a bridge, not a wall.
2. Since there will be no winner or loser, start looking for common ground. These commonalities will become the path linking your side and the other person's side.
3. Refuse to get sucked into "My way or the highway" thinking. Maintain your focus on building the bridge.

4. Words are not the main building blocks of this bridge. The building blocks are silence, compassion, understanding, eye contact, open body language, and a calm, caring presence. Use words sparingly, and only when necessary.

5. Giving, rather than taking, is the best strategy for getting across the bridge. This way, you cross it not with an escort into hostile territory, but with a companion who knows the territory. Rather than a solo activity, this becomes a journey where you face dangers together and discover safety nets that protect you both.

6. Instead of winning an argument, you transform it into an opportunity to destroy animosity and build a bridge of understanding, tolerance and caring.

7. It's possible that once the bridge is built, you decide you don't want to cross it after all. Perhaps that's not the direction you are going. You can change direction without burning the bridge and without spewing verbal "burning coals" all over it. That's OK too. Change direction and leave. Leave in peace.

## Activity

In a small group of four or five people, role play a hot topic conversation between two of you. Choose sides in advance and, if possible, choose a perspective on the hot topic that is not in alignment with what you really believe.

Discuss the topic for two minutes. Then get feedback from the others in the group.

## Lessons Learned: Chart Them and Share

Discuss in small groups the lessons you learned in this chapter. Write your insights on chart paper and share in small groups, then share the best insights in one large group.

**KNOW**

**FEEL**

**ACT**

## Tracking Transformational Actions

What do I **know** now that I didn't know before this training?

What do I **feel** now that I was not aware of feeling before this training?

What must I **act** on to instigate change in myself, my work, and the people with whom I interact?

| Know | Feel | Act |
|---|---|---|
|  |  |  |
|  |  |  |
|  |  |  |
|  |  |  |
|  |  |  |
|  |  |  |
|  |  |  |
|  |  |  |
|  |  |  |

## Quotes

*"Say what you mean, but don't say it mean."*                                    Andrea Wachter, marriage counselor

*"Speak not injurious words, neither in jest or earnest; scoff at none although they give occasion."*
                                                                                    George Washington

*"…we can all have different opinions without demeaning and dehumanizing one another…disagree without being disagreeable."*                                                                  Sally Kohn

# 9. HOLDING ACCOUNTABILITY CONVERSATIONS

## Definition

Accountability is an attitude, an obligation, or a willingness to accept responsibility or to account for one's actions and perhaps the actions of others. It is a willingness to give an account for your actions, to explain them, and to accept the responsibility for the consequences of what you have done.

An accountability conversation is one in which one person attempts to hold another person responsible for something done incorrectly, dangerously, haphazardly, recklessly, or without heed to guidelines and protocols.

### What it is

Accountability conversations address the question, "How did that happen?" (This is also the title of a useful book on accountability listed in the Additional Resources section of this workbook.) These conversations are open and fueled by the "need to know."

Remember that conversation is not supposed to be a competition, and that the need to be right triggers a fierce determination to win rather than a real sense of curiosity to learn more about others and what they want and need. In an accountability conversation, what is more important than being right is to be truly present, to hear what is being said, and to understand what is expected of you (whether you are the one initiating or on the receiving end of an accountability conversation).

### What it isn't

Accountability conversations are not motivated by the need for revenge or to discredit or shame other people. They are not mean-spirited, nor an excuse to dump on someone or try to make the person shrink or melt or just go away. They are not nasty tirades.

# Assessment

Use the Activity below and the feedback you give one another as your assessment.

You will do this exercise twice. Do it once now as an Assessment. Do it again when you get to the Activity section below.

(If you want more feedback after you finish this workbook — and if you have the courage to face getting more feedback, ask your work team or family member, if you dare, to complete the assessment in ***The Power of the Zip*** on your communication strengths and weaknesses (**p. 39** - Self-Assessments-Conversation a). When they give you feedback, use the Job Aid on p. 92, "How to Give and Receive Feedback," as your guide for receiving their feedback.)

## Related Topics in POZ*

*(*The Power of the Zip* book)*

Chapter 8 – The Power of Listening
Chapter 35 – The Power of Being Real
Chapter 9 – The Power of the Question

## Coaching

**Questions to Ask Yourself**

1.   Is this a necessary conversation to have? If so, why?

2.   What is my role in the situation? Explain.

3. Am I prepared to hold the conversation? List the ways you are prepared.

4. How "*SURE*" am I? Explain.

5. What do I need to do to keep my emotions in check?

6. Do I have all of the facts? If you do, what are they?

7. If I played a role in this situation, how do I hold myself accountable?

## Reframe Worksheet

| What I am feeling | What I want to say | What I shouldn't say | What I should say |
|---|---|---|---|
|  |  |  |  |
|  |  |  |  |
|  |  |  |  |
|  |  |  |  |
|  |  |  |  |
|  |  |  |  |
|  |  |  |  |
|  |  |  |  |
|  |  |  |  |

### Questions to Ask Others

1. Can you help me understand …...?
2. How did this happen?
3. If you could do it over again, what measures to improve accountability would you add to your process?
4. What do you want?
5. How will you know when you get it?
6. What do you mean by that?
7. What would it take to return to compliance?
8. How can I support you in this?
9. If you could do this over again, what would you do differently?

### BONUS: Tips to improve your accountability conversations

1. Prepare
   - Face your assumptions, then set them aside
   - Rehearse your perspective, words, and vocal tone
2. Before launching into the conversation, ask, "Do you have a minute?"
3. Make it safe
   - Ask questions with curiosity, do not interrogate
   - Assure the person you are on the same team, then behave that way
4. Decode or "take in" the thoughts and feelings and general demeanor of the other person. He or she may not want to have this conversation or may not know how to have this conversation. If you jump in too quickly, you risk erecting barriers that will be hard to remove.
5. Ask, "What would it take to return to compliance?" Then ZIP it while the other person answers. This alone may solve your accountability problem

- Accountability can be contagious. Let others see what you do to hold yourself accountable.
- Catch people exhibiting accountable behaviors and holding successful accountable conversations. Don't be stingy with positive feedback.

## Activity

With a partner, role-play an accountability conversation.

Select an issue where there was an accountability problem. Take turns asking questions.

Then swap roles and role-play another accountability conversation.

## Lessons Learned: Chart Them and Share

Discuss in small groups the lessons you learned in this chapter. Write your insights on chart paper and share in small groups, then share the best insights in one large group.

## Tracking Transformational Actions

**KNOW**

**FEEL**

**ACT**

What do I **know** now that I didn't know before this training?

What do I **feel** now that I was not aware of feeling before this training?

What must I **act** on to instigate change in myself, my work, and the people with whom I interact?

| Know | Feel | Act |
|------|------|-----|
|      |      |     |
|      |      |     |
|      |      |     |
|      |      |     |
|      |      |     |
|      |      |     |
|      |      |     |
|      |      |     |
|      |      |     |

## Quotes

*"When bad things happen, resist the urge to blame others. Instead, find something you can do yourself to fix the problem."*

Dave Ramsey

*"Accountability breeds response –ability."*

Stephen Covey

# 10. FACILITATING MEETINGS

## Definition

To facilitate a meeting is to make the meeting effective, functional, necessary, successful and not boring. The meeting should be a worthwhile expenditure of time and definitely add value. A facilitator sets the tone for meetings in order to uncover and deal with issues, explore innovations, solve problems, or develop and accept action plans.

Neutrality is important in facilitating a meeting. The facilitator mediates the process without imposing a point of view or having a hidden agenda.

| What it is | What it isn't |
|---|---|
| There is no single formula for a meeting that produces innovative products and/or ideas that add tremendous value to an organization. Worthwhile meetings can be quiet or noisy, with many or few participants, and be short or long. To ensure that the group is using the most effective means of working through the meeting agenda, the facilitator might introduce tools such as brainstorming, creative problem solving, or breakout group discussions. Then in future meetings, take turns facilitating so that everyone has a chance to experience this newly established process. | As a rule, the meetings in which participants sleep or indulge in many side conversations, or when they find the briefings long and boring, tend not to be of value. Any activity or conversation that can take place virtually or with a memo, email, text, or quick phone call should be eliminated from a meeting agenda. Venting, whining, and complaining seldom lead to action. Restrict these displays to private, one-on-one meetings. Don't let these behaviors pollute group settings. If you do, little will be accomplished. |

## Assessment

Think about one of the last meetings you attended or facilitated. Review the guidelines in this chapter and assess how the meeting followed those guidelines.

Make a list for yourself of anything that should have been done differently. If you think the meeting was unnecessary, what activity or process could you have replaced the meeting with. Be specific.

# Related Topics in POZ*

(*The Power of the Zip book)

All chapters

(Note: To be maximally effective, facilitators need to master every aspect of listening and speaking described in POZ.)

# Coaching

**Questions to Ask Yourself**

1. What skills do I need to lead this meeting successfully?

2. How do I determine who must attend this meeting and who can skip it?

3. What action(s) should result from this meeting?

4. How can I instigate creative problem solving?

5. What mistakes did I make in past meetings that I want to avoid this time?

### Reframe Worksheet

| What I am feeling when facilitating a meeting | What I want to say to people who refuse to engage | What I shouldn't say to people who don't deliver results | What I should say when the meeting gets stuck |
|---|---|---|---|
| | | | |
| | | | |
| | | | |
| | | | |
| | | | |
| | | | |
| | | | |
| | | | |
| | | | |

## Questions to Ask Others

1. What role, if any, do you think you should play in this meeting?
2. If you were in charge of this meeting, what would it look like from beginning to end? Please be specific.
3. If you wanted to be a change agent at the meeting, what change would you try to bring about?
4. What mistakes do you see in other meetings that we should avoid here?
5. What new action steps were decided at the meeting? How will they be implemented?

## BONUS: Some facilitation guidelines

- keep the meeting focused on one item at a time until decisions are reached;
- regulate the flow of discussion—draw out quiet people or those with the most relevant expertise, and limit those who tend to talk a lot; assign a timekeeper for each step of the process
- clarify and summarize points, test for consensus, and formalize decisions;
- help the group deal with conflicts;
- keep the meeting running on time;
- ensure the minutes of the meeting list the action points and decisions reached.

Suggested reading: *No More Pointless Meetings* by Martin Murphy

- Use a checklist to track what works and what needs work when you lead a meeting.
- When attending meetings that you don't lead, track what others do that works and what needs to be improved.

## Activity

In a small group, decide on a reason for a meeting. Be clear that the meeting must happen in order for *xxx* to occur. Pick a topic with immediacy, such as, "How to Prepare for an Active Shooter Incident at our Facility."

Plan the agenda and establish the expected outcomes. Make sure action items are clearly spelled out. Assign tasks beforehand.

Set a time limit, e.g., 20-25 minutes, and plan accordingly so that all the allotted time will be used and no one will feel that his/her time has been wasted. Assign the number of minutes to each agenda item.

Assign people to roles: facilitator, minutes taker, time keeper, and attendees. The attendees should be chosen on the basis of who is essential to the purpose of the meeting. Develop criteria to determine who should attend.

## Lessons Learned: Chart Them and Share

Discuss in small groups the lessons you learned in this chapter. Write your insights on chart paper and share in small groups, then share the best insights in one large group.

## Tracking Transformational Actions

KNOW

FEEL

ACT

What do I **know** now that I didn't know before this training?

What do I **feel** now that I was not aware of feeling before this training?

What must I **act** on to instigate change in myself, my work, and the people with whom I interact?

| Know | Feel | Act |
|---|---|---|
|  |  |  |
|  |  |  |
|  |  |  |
|  |  |  |
|  |  |  |
|  |  |  |
|  |  |  |
|  |  |  |
|  |  |  |

## Quotes

*"The fundamental purpose of meetings is to utilize the collective human capital of a group to get things accomplished."*
Martin Murphy

*"Make your meetings the ones that people want to attend: short, necessary and memorable."*     Jill Kamp Melton

# 11. APOLOGIZING THE RIGHT WAY

## Definition

Merriam-Webster's Dictionary defines an apology as "an admission of error or discourtesy accompanied by an expression of regret." It is not a quickly muttered "Sorry." The expression of regret is sincere and accompanied by an assurance to make every effort to ensure it does not recur.

### What it is

An apology is a sincere admission of guilt about something you have said or done that may have hurt others or a process, or some way in which you interfered with others or a process.

It is not just saying, "I'm truly sorry." You must add some understanding of the pain or disruption you caused and how that made you feel and how it might have made others feel. It may also require reparations in words or deeds.

The person apologizing needs to feel serious sorrow for having caused the hurt. And the person to whom the apology is given needs to feel truly validated and helped.

### What it isn't

An apology that is off-handed, emotionless, or insensitive is not an apology. "Sorry," without feelings and sensitivity exacerbates the problem and waters down the gesture.

## Assessment

Take the Communication Style Self-Assessment in *The Power of the Zip*, Chapter 2 - The Power of Perspectives, **p. 16**, to figure out which styles you and those with whom you converse use most frequently. Have you needed to apologize for using any of these styles?

# Related Topics in POZ*

*(\*The Power of the Zip book)*

# Coaching

**Questions to Ask Yourself**

1. What signals might I be missing that are telling me I have hurt someone and need to apologize?

2. What types of situations do I get into that require me to apologize?

3. If I need to apologize to someone, do I feel relieved when I have finished apologizing? Do I feel that I have completely apologized? Does an apology need to be verbal?

## Reframe Worksheet

| What I am feeling when I need to apologize | What I want to say as an apology | What I shouldn't say when apologizing | What I should say in order to heal the hurt I have caused |
|---|---|---|---|
|  |  |  |  |
|  |  |  |  |
|  |  |  |  |
|  |  |  |  |
|  |  |  |  |
|  |  |  |  |
|  |  |  |  |
|  |  |  |  |
|  |  |  |  |

## Questions to Ask Others

1. What seems sincere in the way I apologize?
2. What seems insincere in the way I apologize?
3. If you were to coach me about how to apologize with sincerity and to show vulnerability to others, what would you tell me?

# Context: Personal and Community

## Personal Context

***The Power of the Zip*** lists 10 conversation styles. The most professional style that helps us avoid "even the appearance of wrong doing" is professional and/or thoughtful reasoned conversation.[3] When delivering an apology, you want to use this style in a heartfelt way.

If you need to apologize, it doesn't matter if you are in "relationship jail" and your close friends or family don't want to have anything to do with you, it's up to you to make a start.

Since words can hurt and words can heal, practice the art of apologizing with a clerk in a store, a vendor on the street, or a casual acquaintance, and begin to "use language with the skill of a surgeon and a crisis negotiator."

Here's a possible scenario: You are brusque as you start to checkout your items at the store register. The clerk, however, says, "Hello, and how are you today?" Apologize for your rudeness, abruptness or insensitivity, or whatever other behavior you exhibited that was less than it should have been. Answer with, "I'm so sorry I blurted out my business before greeting you. Hello, how's your day

---

[3] The Power of the Zip, p. 6

been going so far." Then, "These items are on sale and I want to make sure I get the correct price. Please check to see what that is, Thanks for working with me on this." Engage in direct eye contact and muster a smile that says, "I'm glad you are here to help me."

If this way of speaking seems too effusive and relational, don't dismiss it without trying it. You will be amazed by how it changes both the clerk and you. To the clerk, this may be the only sign of respect and validation this person gets all day. It makes a difference to him and, in turn, it makes you a person who cares about helping, not hurting others, all day. When you get out of a "gotta get things done" mindset and start interacting civilly with others, it's not just the lives of other people that you will positively impact; yours will change for the better too.

The more you care about people, the more you will want to interact with others in a way that is careful and hospitable. Communication is not a sudden tornado that rips up the house, leaving the house in need of ongoing repairs and constant damage control. When people are disregarded, they feel, if even for just a moment, like victims in a world over which they have no control.

Professional reasoned conversation is intentional and the result of a desire to be mature in thought, word and deed. So, using some of the other conversational styles, i.e. whining, idle chit chat, gossip, teasing, coarse language, and abusive language, reduces the professional decorum of conversation. When you use these styles, you are more prone to getting into situations for which you will need to apologize.

## Community Context

At the time of this writing (2018), the need for corporate and personal apologies in the United States seems intense. Many groups of people who feel they have been seriously invalidated or even violated crave sincere apologies that are never delivered. These include descendants of slaves, descendants of Holocaust victims and survivors, relatives of people held in internment camps after World War II, employees of businesses that went bankrupt who lost money, time and reputations. The list of people who want validation, apologies, consideration, and reparation seems endless.

When governments and corporations do not apologize in a sincere way to people who feel victimized, the pain of that injury can have a corrosive effect on families and society.

That's why mastering the skill of apology is so imperative. This requires that we understand who got hurt, how that happened, and what role we played. The vital components of an apology that would be acceptable to the recipient are: speaking words of true repentance, expressing feelings that reflect heartfelt remorse, and conveying an assurance that no anger is harbored. When appropriate or necessary, reparation should be made.

If leaders don't address the issues and actions that have hurt people, and if they and/or the perpetrators don't apologize in a way that victims accept as meaningful, the result is a toxic atmosphere that is almost impossible to eradicate. It is up to leaders to remove their blind spots, just as ophthalmologists remove cataracts, so people who are going blind can see again. Leaders must cultivate an attentiveness to the hurts that an organization drags around like a ball and chain. To do this successfully, leaders must practice until they become skilled at the art of the apology. Once they have harnessed its power, they become role models for others.

---

### Key Question to Consider

*When you are giving a sincere apology and feel vulnerable, how do you handle it?*

---

- Leaders think displaying emotion and vulnerability are out of place at work. This is wrong-headed thinking.
- An apology out of obligation will sound shallow and can further damage already damaged relationships. An apology delivered from true depth of feeling builds bridges and heals damaged relationships.

## Activity

Select a topic or situation that you witnessed or participated in that required an apology afterwards. With a partner and using professional and thoughtful reasoned conversation, practice giving an apology to the other person.

Switch roles.

Now give feedback: First, give feedback on how you think you did, then get feedback from your partner.

Switch and listen to your partner's feedback about himself/herself, then give him or her your feedback.

Make sure you evaluate sincerity, how assured you feel that the behavior won't occur again, and whether or not honest remorse and a willingness to make reparations were expressed.

## Lessons Learned: Chart Them and Share

Discuss in small groups the lessons you learned in this chapter. Write your insights on chart paper and share in small groups, then share the best insights in one large group.

KNOW

FEEL

ACT

## Tracking Transformational Actions

What do I **know** now that I didn't know before this training?

What do I **feel** now that I was not aware of feeling before this training?

What must I **act** on to instigate change in myself, my work, and the people with whom I interact?

| Know | Feel | Act |
|------|------|-----|
|      |      |     |
|      |      |     |
|      |      |     |
|      |      |     |
|      |      |     |
|      |      |     |
|      |      |     |
|      |      |     |
|      |      |     |

# Quotes

*"Never ruin an apology with an excuse."*                                        Unknown

*"An apology given just to appease one's conscience is self-serving and better left unspoken!"*        Evinda Lepins

*"Any good apology has 3 parts: 1) I'm sorry 2) It's my fault 3) What can I do to make it right? Most people forget the third part."*                                        Unknown

*"You can always say sorry, But the real apology is when you hear the sadness in their voice and see the look in their eyes. And you realize that they have hurt themselves just as much."*        *Kid Cudi*

*"When we don't apologize, we have arrested development. The purpose of an apology is to repair what has been broken."*        *Allan H. Gray*

# 12. DEVELOPING A LEADERSHIP EDGE

## Definition

A leader is the one entrusted with the responsibility to fulfill a mission and do it in concert with others. Final decisions ultimately reside with a leader, and he or she is accountable for the mission's successful or failure.

It's been said that if you are a leader and no one is following you, you are just a person out for a walk.

Leaders are also role models for those they lead. If they fail, they are a role model of failure. If they succeed, others will want to follow their example and replicate their success.

### What it is

Leaders who are intentional about leaving a legacy worth something are careful. They seek out exceptional mentors and role models and continually look to acquire wisdom and learn to exercise caution. Self-control and maturity are their goals and they ask for and receive feedback with humility and interest in self-improvement.

### What it isn't

Leaders who don't care about their legacy engage in reckless speech or behaviors and make reckless decisions. They choose friends and colleagues out of selfish ambition and an insatiable need for fun and adventure. Their decisions are unsound and they don't seem to care.

## Assessment

Read George Washington's "Rules of Civility & Decent Behaviour" on p. 99 and circle all the rules that you violate. Write them into plain language and develop an action plan to improve.

Discuss a few of these with a small group. Try to figure out what makes you do these things.

# Related Topics in POZ*

*(*The Power of the Zip book)*

# Coaching

**Questions to Ask Yourself**

1. How do I follow other leaders?

2. What kind of follow-ship do I model?

3. How do I like to be validated?

4. How do they like to be validated – how would I know?

5.  How do I like to be contacted?

6.  How do they like to be contacted – how would I know?

7.  What change do I think is the highest priority for my organization?

8.  How can I inspire greater employee engagement?

9.  Do I perpetuate the silos in my organization? If so, how?

10. How can I inspire my workforce to think about teambuilding instead of insulating the silo?

## Reframe Worksheet

| What I am feeling as I lead others | How I want to behave as a leader | How I shouldn't behave as a leader | How I should behave |
|---|---|---|---|
| | | | |
| | | | |
| | | | |
| | | | |
| | | | |
| | | | |
| | | | |
| | | | |
| | | | |

### Questions to Ask Others

1. Do you track your legacy? If so, how? If not, how might you do it?
2. Solicit feedback about your legacy. Ask, "How do you think I'm doing in my job?"
3. What should I be doing differently?
4. What self-knowledge do you think is lacking in our workforce?
5. What denials of reality do you think infect our organization?
6. What are we doing about relationship repair within our group?

---

### Key Question to Consider

*As a role model, what do you need to change about yourself
so that you don't mislead others?*

---

- Everyone is a role model for someone. Who do you think uses you as a role model?
- Who are your role models? Take account of what you learn and copy from them. Review the list occasionally to see where you need to improve.

# Activity

Define your legacy: Think about what would you like to be remembered for when you leave your organization. Write your thoughts and ideas below.

In small groups of 3 or 4 people, each person shares for 2 minutes about a legacy a role model left for him or her. Talk about what the role model did, the impact that it had on you and on the organization, and what you want to replicate in your career.

## Lessons Learned: Chart Them and Share

Discuss in small groups the lessons you learned in this chapter. Write your insights on chart paper and share in small groups, then share the best insights in one large group.

KNOW

FEEL

ACT

## Tracking Transformational Actions

What do I **know** now that I didn't know before this training?

What do I **feel** now that I was not aware of feeling before this training?

What must I **act** on to instigate change in myself, my work, and the people with whom I interact?

| Know | Feel | Act |
| --- | --- | --- |
|  |  |  |
|  |  |  |
|  |  |  |
|  |  |  |
|  |  |  |
|  |  |  |
|  |  |  |
|  |  |  |
|  |  |  |

## Quotes

from *The Leadership Playbook* by Jill Kamp Melton

*"Under-promise and over-deliver."*

*"When necessary, say 'I'm on deadline' and mean it."*

*"When enticed to gossip, declare, 'I'm not going to play.'"*

*"Avoid even the appearance of wrongdoing."*

A sign on a road in Vermont says, *"Choose your rut carefully because you will be in it for the next 20 miles."*

*"If 50,000 people say a stupid thing, it is still a stupid thing."*

Anatole France

*"Go to a funeral to learn how to live."*

Jill Kamp Melton

# 13. MANAGING STRESS

## Definition

Stress is a psychological state of being that alerts us to get help or tells us that we are about to accomplish great things. Wisdom is knowing the difference. Stress it is part of the human condition, but when we are beset by multiple thoughts and feelings and impulses that do not promote inner peace, too much stress debilitates us.

### What it is

When we experience "good" stress, our mind, heart, actions, and very essence are mobilized around a task or a creative discovery that is an altogether new experience for us, and perhaps for others also. We are energized, hopeful, focused, and thrilled by the new experience.

### What it isn't

When we are overwhelmed by too many thoughts, feelings, and events in our lives and/or the lives around us, we can become manic or depressed, look morose, and obsess about the futility of life. This type of stress is uncomfortable for us and for those around us. We might express distress outwardly by fussing, fuming and arguing. We might also tremble, cry, or feel empty and edgy.

## Assessments

These two assessments in **The Power of The Zip** will highlight for you what behaviors you exhibit when you are stressed. Managing your stress will help reduce speaking and acting in reckless ways.

- Chapter 6 – The Power of Wait, **p. 40**
- Chapter 10 – The Power of Words, **p. 64** - How You Use Language-A

# Related Topics in POZ*

*(\*The Power of the Zip book)*

Chapter 29 – The Power of the Smile
Chapter 32 – The Power of Etiquette and Tact
Chapter 34 – The Power of Emotion

# Coaching

**Questions to Ask Yourself**

1. How do I handle myself when I recognize emotions in me like anger, stubbornness, rebelliousness, envy, and/or exasperation, or behaviors like trembling, being rude to and/or rough with others, acting scattered, or states of being like wanting to cry, feeling rushed and/or overwhelmed, and/or feeling sick, edgy, empty and/or shallow?

2. If I wanted help handling these uncomfortable states of being, what should I do? Use the Reframe Worksheet **on the next page** to organize your thoughts.

## Reframe Worksheet

| Stressors | Current Behavior | Current Attitudes | New Plan | New Attitudes |
|---|---|---|---|---|
| Relaxation | | | | |
| Time Management | | | | |
| Living Situation | | | | |
| Stamina | | | | |
| Organization | | | | |
| What I eat | | | | |
| Money Management | | | | |
| Knowing what makes me glad | | | | |
| Knowing what makes me mad | | | | |
| Knowing what makes me sad | | | | |
| Knowing what makes me bad | | | | |

## Questions to Ask Others

1. What would it take for you to take care of yourself?
2. What areas of your professional life need better care?
3. What areas of your personal life need better care?
4. When under stress, how can you incorporate the HALT strategies (hungry, angry, lonely, tired) below in each of these areas?
   a. When you are hungry, eat something good for you. Ditch the sugar and add more fresh fruits and vegetables to your diet.
   b. Anger is a secondary emotion. Usually we are angry with ourselves but that emotion can seem so overwhelming, that we try to dump the anger on others. Forgive yourself and forgive others even when we and they don't deserve it.

c.  People are meant to have relationships with others. Decide how much or how little you need and get your daily "relationship fix." None is not an acceptable answer.

d.  Most people don't get enough sleep. Inventory your time wasters and eliminate them one by one. You will have more time to sleep and more time to reflect. Sleep and reflection are vitamins for the spirit and the body. They build us up, especially when we experience lots of stress.

---

## Key Question to Consider
*To minimize stress in your life, what adjustments do you have to make?*

---

- It is easier to pinpoint and diagnose the stress in someone else's life than in our own.
- Partnering with someone to help you be accountable when stressed is very healthy.

## Activity

Select one of the following quotes and explain to a small group how it applies to you and the stress in your life. Invite the group to ask you clarifying questions.

1.  "To be nobody, but myself, in a world which is doing its best day and night, to make you everybody else – means to fight the hardest battle which any human being can fight, and never stop fighting."
    E.E. Cummings

2.  "Never mistake motion for action."               Ernest Hemingway

3.  "No one can make you feel inferior without your consent."      Eleanor Roosevelt

4.  There is no bad weather, only bad clothing."        Norwegian proverb

5.  "Fail to prepare, prepare to fail."                Unknown

6.  "Live in expectation that this time will be different."      Jill Kamp Melton

7.  "It's not how much money you spend that counts but how you spend what you have that matters."                                                        Jill Kamp Melton

8.  "Learn from your mistakes."                                                        Jill Kamp Melton

9.  "Most of the time, less is more."                                                        Jill Kamp Melton

10. "Silence can be noisy if it is impatient. Patient silence is quiet."                                                        Jill Kamp Melton

11. "Just because you said something doesn't mean it was heard."                                                        Jill Kamp Melton

12. "Sometimes our enemies do us favors that they did not intend."                                                        Jill Kamp Melton

13. "I have decided to speak out in the hope that we can come together as Americans, and through peaceful dialogue and education, achieve constructive change."                                                        Michael Jordan

14. "I have seen how inadequate my own words have been."                                                        Barack Obama

15. "Everyone should focus on words that unite."                                                        Barack Obama

16. "Too often we judge other groups by their worst examples while judging ourselves by our best intentions."                                                        George W. Bush

17. "Drawing on my fine command of the English language, I said nothing."                                                        Robert Benchley

18. "Not merely an absence or noise, real silence begins when a reasonable being withdraws from the noise in order to find peace and order in his inner sanctuary."                                                        Peter Minard

19. "We do not see things as they are. We see things as we are."                                                        Rabbi Shemuel ben Nachmani

20. "One of the symptoms of an approaching nervous breakdown is the belief that one's work is terribly important."                                                        Bertrand Russell

21. "The greatest weapon against stress is our ability to choose one thought over another."                                                        William James

22. "When you find yourself stressed, ask yourself one question: Will this matter in 5 years from now? If yes, then do something about the situation. If no, then let it go."                                                        Catherine Pulsifer

23. "Do not anticipate trouble or worry about what may never happen. Keep in the sunlight."

Marcus Aurelius

## BONUS: Prescription to reduce stress

**RENEW** yourself

- **R**ead: be inspired by role models who have written about their lives and their work. Aim to read at least one new book a month.

- **E**xamine: use the assessments in this workbook to discover what works and what you need to do differently.

- **N**ew goals: identify them, write them down and share them with at least one person. Commit to your new direction.

- **E**xpect the best; prepare for the worst. Under promise and over deliver. Exercise your body, your mind, and your spirit every single day.

- **W**ork with the expectation that what you do will matter to others. Look for the fruit of that expectation. When you see it, write it down.

**REFRESH** yourself:

- **R**eality: get in touch with who you really are so you can use your strengths and keep your weaknesses from getting in the way. Get real, and work on feeling comfortable in your own skin.

- **E**ncourage: encourage yourself and encourage others

- **F**eel / **F**orgive / **F**ree / **F**riends: don't block your emotions; forgive others even when they don't deserve it; free yourself from emotional baggage and toxic relationships; cultivate friends who are positive, vibrant and have a sense of humor

- **R**ebuild **r**adically: rebuild your life with courage to try radical, positive, healthy new ways of thinking and being

- **E**ndure: hang in there when the going gets tough without being rough on yourself and others

- **S**elf-control: a mature person exercises self-discipline and self-control

- **H**andle / **H**eal / **H**ealthy: handle your problems with a clear mind and heart. Heal what is not healthy about you, and works towards renewed health every day and in every way.

# Lessons Learned: Chart Them and Share

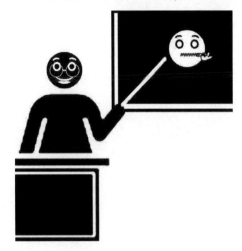

Discuss in small groups the lessons you learned in this chapter. Write your insights on chart paper and share in small groups, then share the best insights in one large group.

| KNOW |
|:---:|
| FEEL |
| ACT |

## Tracking Transformational Actions

What do I **know** now that I didn't know before this training?

What do I **feel** now that I was not aware of feeling before this training?

What must I **act** on to instigate change in myself, my work, and the people with whom I interact?

| Know | Feel | Act |
|---|---|---|
|  |  |  |
|  |  |  |
|  |  |  |
|  |  |  |
|  |  |  |
|  |  |  |
|  |  |  |
|  |  |  |
|  |  |  |

## Quote

*"It's not the load that breaks you down, it's the way you carry it."*                    Lou Holtz

# REVIEW

## When to Zip It Checklist

Check the descriptions that may have been true for you in the past.
Use this checklist often as a reminder to avoid meddling at all costs.

| Strategies for Living Unlimited List | Any more to add? |
|---|---|
| When you are angry | |
| Before you have all the facts | |
| When you are supposed to be working | |
| When you repeat yourself on an issue over and over again | |
| When you are tempted to flatter someone who is flat out wrong in order to get favors | |
| When there is a chance your words will offend someone | |
| Before you have mastered your feelings and your perspective | |
| If you would not want a video of this interaction on YouTube | |
| When you are tempted to joke about hot topics | |
| When you probably will regret later what you said and how you said it | |
| If there is a chance that you might leave a wrong impression | |
| If you are meddling and the issue really is not yours to deal with | |
| If you might be stretching the truth or lying | |
| If your words might be construed as slander | |
| If the interaction could kill a relationship | |
| If you are in a judgmental, critical mood | |
| If you are tempted to yell | |
| When you should be listening instead of talking | |

If you seriously believe that you need to take the opportunity to have a particular conversation (rather than to zip it), double check with a mentor and/or peer to make sure you will add value by doing so and not destroy a relationship and/or a process.

# JOB AID

## 13 Signs of High Emotional Intelligence

By Justin Bariso [4]

Wonder what emotional intelligence looks like in everyday life? Here are 13 examples.

In 1995, psychologist and science journalist Daniel Goleman published a book introducing most of the world to the nascent concept of emotional intelligence. The idea--that an ability to understand and manage emotions greatly increases our chances of success--quickly took off, and it went on to greatly influence the way people think about emotions and human behavior.
But what does emotional intelligence look like, as manifested in everyday life?

For the past two years, I've explored that question in researching my forthcoming book, *EQ, Applied*. In doing so, I've identified a number of actions that illustrate how emotional intelligence appears in the real world.
Here are 13 of them:

### 1. You think about feelings.

Emotional intelligence begins with what is called self- and social awareness, the ability to recognize emotions (and their impact) in both yourself and others.
That awareness begins with reflection. You ask questions like:
* What are my emotional strengths? What are my weaknesses?
* How does my current mood affect my thoughts and decision making?
* What's going on under the surface that influences what others say or do?
Pondering questions like these yield valuable insights that can be used to your advantage.

### 2. You pause.

The pause is as simple as taking a moment to stop and think before you speak or act. (Easy in theory, difficult in practice.) This can help save you from embarrassing moments or from making commitments too quickly.
In other words, pausing helps you refrain from making a permanent decision based on a temporary emotion.

### 3. You strive to control your thoughts.

You don't have much control over the emotion you experience in a given moment. But you can control your reaction to those emotions--by focusing on your thoughts. (As it's been said: You can't

---

[4] Reprinted with permission from the author
Justin Bariso is the author of EQ Applied, which shares fascinating research, modern examples, and personal stories to illustrate how emotional intelligence works in the real world – and gives practical tips for building yours.

Use this link to access his book: https://www.amazon.com/dp/B07D7K9386/

prevent a bird from landing on your head, but you *can* keep it from building a nest.)

By striving to control your thoughts, you resist becoming a slave to your emotions, allowing yourself to live in a way that's in harmony with your goals and values.

### 4. You benefit from criticism.

Nobody enjoys negative feedback. But you know that criticism is a chance to learn, even if it's not delivered in the best way. And even when it's unfounded, it gives you a window into how others think.

When you receive negative feedback, you keep your emotions in check and ask yourself: How can this make me better?

### 5. You show authenticity.

Authenticity doesn't mean sharing everything about yourself, to everyone, all of the time. It *does* mean saying what you mean, meaning what you say, and sticking to your values and principles above all else.

You know not everyone will appreciate your sharing your thoughts and feelings. But the ones who matter will.

### 6. You demonstrate empathy.

The ability to show empathy, which includes understanding others' thoughts and feelings, helps you connect with others. Instead of judging or labeling others, you work hard to see things through their eyes.

Empathy doesn't necessarily mean agreeing with another person's point of view. Rather, it's about striving to understand--which allows you to build deeper, more connected relationships.

### 7. You praise others.

All humans crave acknowledgement and appreciation. When you commend others, you satisfy that craving and build trust in the process.

This all begins when you focus on the good in others. Then, by sharing specifically what you appreciate, you inspire them to be the best version of themselves.

### 8. You give helpful feedback.

Negative feedback has great potential to hurt the feelings of others. Realizing this, you reframe criticism as constructive feedback, so the recipient sees it as helpful instead of harmful.

### 9. You apologize.

It takes strength and courage to be able to say you're sorry. But doing so demonstrates humility, a quality that will naturally draw others to you.

Emotional intelligence helps you realize that apologizing doesn't always mean you're wrong. It *does* mean valuing your relationship more than your ego.

### 10. You forgive and forget.

Hanging on to resentment is like leaving a knife inside a wound. While the offending party moves on with their life, you never give yourself the chance to heal.

When you forgive and forget, you prevent others from holding your emotions hostage--allowing you to move forward.

### 11. You keep your commitments.

It's common nowadays for people to break an agreement or commitment when they feel like it. Of course, bailing on an evening of Netflix with a friend will cause less harm than breaking a promise to your child or missing a major business deadline.

But when you make a habit of keeping your word--in things big and small--you develop a strong reputation for reliability and trustworthiness.

### 12. You help others.

One of the greatest ways to positively impact the emotions of others is to help them.

Most people don't really care where you graduated from, or even about your previous accomplishments. But what about the hours you're willing to take out of your schedule to listen or help out? Your readiness to get down in the trenches and work alongside them?

Actions like these build trust and inspire others to follow your lead when it counts.

### 13. You protect yourself from emotional sabotage.

You realize that emotional intelligence also has a dark side--such as when individuals attempt to manipulate others' emotions to promote a personal agenda or for some other selfish cause.

And that's why you continue to sharpen your own emotional intelligence--to protect yourself when they do.

# JOB AID
## How to Give and Receive Feedback

### Giving Feedback

1. Use "I" statements.
2. Describe behaviors, not the person.
3. Be non-evaluative and non-judgmental (good/bad, right/wrong).
4. Be specific and direct.
5. Direct the feedback toward behavior that the recipient can change.
6. Offer options or reinforce behavior.
7. After feedback has been given
   a. Check with the recipient to find out how he or she heard and/or understood it.
   b. Identify alternative behaviors (if appropriate and requested).


### Receiving Feedback

1. Understand what was said.
2. Be open.
3. Check the "fit."
4. Ask for suggestions.
5. Separate yourself from your behavior.
6. Say "Thank you."


### Tips for Requesting Feedback

1. Your main job is to listen. Avoid interjecting, interrupting, defending yourself, or justifying your actions.
2. Don't hold anything against the person giving you feedback, even if you don't like what you hear.

**Feedback Help**

Words that are or are not helpful when giving feedback. Use the blank spaces at the end of the list to write in your own as you discover helpful and not helpful ways of giving feedback.

| Helpful Words | Words that are Not helpful |
|---|---|
| Confident | Nice |
| Creative | Good |
| Comfortable with ambiguity | I liked it |
| Sincere | Awkward |
| Focused | Shallow |
| Centered | Stubborn |
| Open | Manipulator |
| Agile | Moody |
| Hopeful | Pressured |
| Inconsistent | Controlling |
| Humorous | Hostile |
| Discerning | Phony |
| Specific | Vague |
| Easy to follow | Rambling |
| Engaging | Boring |

Some examples of helpful feedback:
- When you redirected the focus of the group, our interpersonal conflicts seemed less important than working together.
- When you switched your tactics several times, I began to be concerned. What was going on?
- When you paraphrased and floundered, I wondered what you were thinking about.
- Your confidence in your process helped us feel confident that we were working well together.
- When you ask questions to coach others, you inspire self-reflection and understanding. It helps others to grow. Thank you.

# JOB AID

## Types of Questions and How to Use Them

| Goal | Type of Inquiry | Examples |
|---|---|---|
| Identify a definitive answer | **Closed**: Inquiries that have a limited set of responses | Did you just buy this product at the register? |
| Explore Data | **Open**: Inquiries that allow for a broad range of answers | "What leads you to conclude that?" <br> "What data do you have for that?" <br> "What causes you to say that?" |
| Generate dialogue, options, or opinions | **Open**: Inquiries that allow for a broad range of answers | "Where do you see this going?" <br> "What are the implications of this decision?" <br> "How do you see it differently?" |
| Solicit additional information | **Probing**: Short inquiries that encourage the speaker to elaborate | "What else?" <br> "What more could you say about that?" <br> "In what way?" |
| Explore reasoning | **Open**: Inquiries that allow for a broad range of answers | "How did you arrive at this conclusion?" <br> "What is the significance of that?" <br> "How does this relate to your other concerns?" |
| Verify emotions | **Reflect**: Inquiries to check accuracy when restating the emotion of the other person's message | "Is it that this decision has hurt you?" <br> "You sound angry. Are you?" <br> "So, you're both really frustrated?" |
| Verify understanding | **Paraphrase**: Inquiries to check accuracy by restating the content of the other person's message | "Are you saying…?" <br> "If I understand correctly, your main concern is…" <br> "Let me see if I got all the facts right……" <br> "What happened was…. Did I miss anything?" |

| Goal | Type of Inquiry | Examples |
|------|-----------------|----------|
| Encourage creativity | **Hypothetical:** Inquiries that require future based answers; may be fact-based or illogical | "What if….?" <br> "What would you do if you could do anything?" <br> "If you were the boss, how would you organize the work?" <br> "If you were me, what would you be thinking right now?" |
| Explore options and plans | **Open:** Inquiries that allow for a broad range of answers | "What's the worst thing that could happen?" <br> "How can we avoid the pitfalls in this plan?" |
| Empower others to resolve issues/problems | **Open:** Inquiries that allow for a broad range of answers | "What would need to happen for you to make this work?" <br> "What's missing for you?" <br> "What would you like to say to him that you haven't said?" <br> "How are others handling this problem?" |
| Ask for feedback and for self-reflection | **Open:** Inquiries that allow for a broad range of answers | "How might I have handled this situation so that you would be more comfortable and not feel threatened?" <br> "If you could go back, what might you do differently?" |

# JOB AID

## Steps to Active Listening and Seven Roadblocks to Communication

### 13 Steps to Better Active Listening

The 13 skills below can help you become a better active listener. You do not have to become adept at all of them to be a good active listener, but the more steps you use, the better you'll be at it. If you use even just three or four of these skills, you will find yourself listening more actively and hearing more of what other people are saying to you.

### 1. Restating

To show you are listening, repeat every so often what you think the person said — not by parroting, but by paraphrasing in your own words what you heard. For example, "Let's see if I'm clear about this. . ."

### 2. Summarizing

Bring together the facts and pieces of the problem to check understanding. For example, "So it sounds to me as if . . ." Or, "Is that it?"

### 3. Encouraging

Use brief, positive prompts to keep the conversation going and show you are listening. For example, "umm-hmmm," "Oh?" "I understand," "Then?" "And?"

### 4. Reflecting

Instead of just repeating, reflect the speaker's words in terms of feelings. For example, "This seems really important to you. . ." **Caution: Don't label other people's feelings unless you are good at it. Practice this one before using.**

### 5. Giving feedback

This lets the person know what your initial thoughts are on the situation. First, ask for permission to give feedback. If he or she agrees, make sure the feedback is about: what you have seen and heard and the impact that it has had. Share pertinent information, observations, insights, and experiences. Then listen carefully to confirm.

## 6. Labeling emotions

Putting feelings into words often will help a person to see things more objectively. To help the person begin, use "door openers" such as, "I'm sensing that you're feeling frustrated/worried/anxious. . ."

## 7. Drawing someone out without conducting an investigation

Use questions to draw a person out and get deeper and more meaningful information from him or her. For example, "What do you think would happen if you. . .?"

## 8. Validating

Acknowledge the person's problems, issues, and feelings. Listen openly and with empathy, and respond in an interested way. For example, "I appreciate your willingness to talk about such a difficult issue. . ." Or, "Wow! I see that you have a lot of passion about that."

## 9. Using pause effectively

Deliberately pause at key points so that the person speaking can take all the time needed to process thoughts, words and responses. It shows that you are not rushing him or her, but rather are allowing the person to set his or her own pace.

## 10. Staying silent

Allow for comfortable silences to slow down the exchange. Give the person speaking time to think as well as talk. Silence can also be very helpful in diffusing an unproductive interaction. Silence also allows both people in the conversation to catch up with what is being said and with their own feelings about the subject.

## 11. Using "I" messages

By using "I" in your statements, you focus on the problem rather than on the person speaking. An I-message can diffuse a potentially hostile interaction. For example, "I am wondering about the intensity of the emotion you are expressing. Please tell me what led up to this so I can follow you."

## 12. Redirecting or taking a time out

If the person speaking is showing signs of being overly aggressive, agitated, or angry, this is the time to shift the discussion to another topic.

## 13. Consequences

Part of the feedback may involve talking about the possible consequences of inaction. Take your cues from what the person is saying. For example, "What happened the last time you stopped taking the medicine your doctor prescribed?" When the person speaking figures out for himself/herself the consequences of his or her actions, it is more powerful than you telling him or her.

## Seven Roadblocks to Communication

These roadblocks to communication can stop a conversation dead in its tracks:
 1. "Why" questions. They tend to make people defensive.

2. Quick reassurances. They are shallow and indicate that you are shutting down the person speaking instead of helping him or her open up. So, avoid saying things like, "Don't worry about that."

3. Advising. Saying things like, "I think you should do xyz," takes the initiative away from the person speaking., You are verbally shutting a door and trying to force the person speaking to walk through a different door.

4. Digging for information and forcing someone to talk about something they would rather not talk about.

5. Being patronizing. It shows a lack of respect, so when you say things like, "You poor thing, I know just how you feel," it can cause hostility instead of openness.

6. Preaching. People feel judged when they hear preachy comments, which can start with words like, "You should. . ." or, "You shouldn't. . ."

7. Interrupting. This shows you aren't interested in what the person is saying.

# George Washington's[5]
# Rules of Civility and Decent Behaviour

*"...and it may truly be said, that never did nature and fortune combine more perfectly to make a man great."*

George Washington to Thomas Jefferson, about 1814

By age sixteen, George Washington had copied out by hand, 110 rules of Civility & Decent Behaviour in Company and Conversation. They are based on a set of rules composed by French Jesuits in 1595. Presumably they were copied out as part of an exercise in penmanship assigned by young Washington's schoolmaster. The first English translations of the French rules appeared in 1640, and are ascribed to Francis Hawkins, the twelve-year-old son of a doctor.

(The manuscript of Washington's handwritten copy can be viewed online here: http://gwpapers.virginia.edu/documents_gw/civility/civil_01.html)

Richard Brookhiser, in his book on Washington wrote, "all modern manners in the western world were originally aristocratic. Courtesy meant behavior appropriate to a court; chivalry comes from chevalier - a knight. Yet Washington was to dedicate himself to freeing America from a court's control. Could manners survive the operation? Without realizing it, the Jesuits who wrote them, and the young man who copied them, were outlining and absorbing a system of courtesy appropriate to equals and near-equals. When the company for whom the decent behavior was to be performed expanded to the nation, Washington was ready. Parson Weems got this right, when he wrote that it was 'no wonder everybody honored him who honored everybody.'"

## The Rules

1.  Every Action done in Company, ought to be with Some Sign of Respect, to those that are Present.

2.  When in Company, put not your Hands to any Part of the Body, not usually Discovered.

3.  Show Nothing to your friend that may affright him.

4.  In the Presence of Others Sing not to yourself with a humming Noise, nor Drum with your Fingers or Feet.

5.  If You Cough, Sneeze, Sigh, or Yawn, do it not Loud but Privately; and Speak not in your Yawning, but put Your handkerchief or Hand before your face and turn aside.

6.  Sleep not when others Speak, Sit not when others stand, Speak not when you Should hold your Peace, walk not on when others Stop.

---

[5] Adapted from https://managers.usc.edu/files/2015/05/George-Washingtons-Rules.pdf and http://gwpapers.virginia.edu/documents_gw/civility/civility_transcript.html. Accessed May 15, 2018

7. Put not off your Cloths in the presence of Others, nor go out your Chamber half Dressed.

8. At Play and at Fire its Good manners to Give Place to the last comer, and affect not to Speak Louder than Ordinary.

9. Spit not in the Fire, nor Stoop low before it neither Put your Hands into the Flames to warm them, nor Set your Feet upon the Fire especially if there be meat before it.

10. When you Sit down, Keep your Feet firm and Even, without putting one on the other or Crossing them.

11. Shift not yourself in the Sight of others nor Gnaw your nails.

12. Shake not the head, Feet, or Legs roll not the Eyes lift not one eyebrow higher than the other wry not the mouth, and bedew no man's face with your Spittle, by approaching too near him [when] you Speak.

13. Kill no Vermin as Fleas, lice ticks &c in the Sight of Others, if you See any filth or thick Spittle put your foot Dexteriously upon it if it be upon the Cloths of your Companions, Put it off privately, and if it be upon your own Cloths return Thanks to him who puts it off.

14. Turn not your Back to others especially in Speaking, Jog not the Table or Desk on which Another reads or writes, lean not upon any one.

15. Keep your Nails clean and Short, also your Hands and Teeth Clean yet without Showing any great Concern for them.

16. Do not Puff up the Cheeks, Loll not out the tongue rub the Hands, or beard, thrust out the lips, or bite them or keep the Lips too open or too Close.

17. Be no Flatterer, neither Play with any that delights not to be Played Withal.

18. Read no Letters, Books, or Papers in Company but when there is a Necessity for the doing of it you must ask leave: come not near the Books or Writings of Another so as to read them unless desired or give your opinion of them unasked also look not nigh when another is writing a Letter.

19. Let your Countenance be pleasant but in Serious Matters Somewhat grave.

20. The Gestures of the Body must be Suited to the discourse you are upon.

21. Reproach none for the Infirmities of Nature, nor Delight to Put them that have in mind thereof.

22. Show not yourself glad at the Misfortune of another though he were your enemy.

23. When you see a Crime punished, you may be inwardly Pleased; but always show Pity to the Suffering Offender.

24. Do not laugh too loud or too much at any Public Spectacle.

25. Superfluous Complements and all Affectation of Ceremony are to be avoided, yet where due they are not to be Neglected.

26. In Pulling off your Hat to Persons of Distinction, as Noblemen, Justices, Churchmen &c make a Reverence, bowing more or less according to the Custom of the Better Bred, and Quality of the Person. Amongst your equals expect not always that they Should begin with you first, but to Pull off the Hat when there is no need is Affectation, in the Manner of Saluting and re-saluting in words keep to the most usual Custom.

27. Tis ill manners to bid one more eminent than yourself be covered as well as not to do it to whom it's due Likewise he that makes too much haste to Put on his hat does not well, yet he ought to Put it on at the first, or at most the Second time of being asked; now what is herein Spoken, of Qualification in behaviour in Saluting, ought also to be observed in taking of Place, and Sitting down for ceremonies without Bounds is troublesome.

28. If any one come to Speak to you while you are Sitting Stand up though he be your Inferiour, and when you Present Seats let it be to every one according to his Degree.

29. When you meet with one of Greater Quality than yourself, Stop, and retire especially if it be at a Door or any Straight place to give way for him to Pass.

30. In walking the highest Place in most Countries Seems to be on the right hand therefore Place yourself on the left of him whom you desire to Honour: but if three walk together the middle Place is the most Honourable the wall is usually given to the most worthy if two walk together.

31. If any one far Surpasses others, either in age, Estate, or Merit [yet] would give Place to a meaner than himself in his own lodging or elsewhere] the one ought not to except it, So he on the other part should not use much earnestness nor offer] it above once or twice.

32. To one that is your equal, or not much inferior you are to give the chief Place in your Lodging and he to who 'tis offered ought at the first to refuse it but at the Second to accept though not without acknowledging his own unworthiness.

33. They that are in Dignity or in office have in all places Precedence but whilst they are Young they ought to respect those that are their equals in Birth or other Qualities, though they have no Public charge.

34. It is good Manners to prefer them to whom we Speak before ourselves especially if they be above us with whom in no Sort we ought to begin.

35. Let your Discourse with Men of Business be Short and Comprehensive.

36. Artificers & Persons of low Degree ought not to use many ceremonies to Lords, or Others of high Degree but Respect and highly Honour them, and those of high Degree ought to treat them with affability & Courtesy, without Arrogance.

37. In Speaking to men of Quality do not lean nor Look them full in the Face, nor approach too near them at least Keep a full Pace from them.

38. In visiting the Sick, do not Presently play the Physician if you be not Knowing therein.

39. In writing or Speaking, give to every Person his due Title According to his Degree & the Custom of the Place.

40. Strive not with your Superiors in argument, but always Submit your Judgment to others with Modesty.

41. Undertake not to Teach your equal in the art himself Professes; it Savours of arrogance.

42. Let thy ceremonies in Courtesy be proper to the Dignity of his place [with whom thou converses] for it is absurd to ac]t the same with a Clown and a Prince.

43. Do not express Joy before one sick or in pain for that contrary Passion will aggravate his Misery.

44. When a man does all he can though it Succeeds not well, blame not him that did it.

45. Being to advise or reprehend any one, consider whether it ought to be in public or in Private; presently, or at Some other time in what terms to do it & in reproving Show no Sign of Choler but do it with all Sweetness and Mildness.

46. Take all Admonitions thankfully in what Time or Place o ever given but afterwards not being culpable take a Time & Place convenient to let him know it that gave them.

47. Mock not nor Jest at any thing of Importance break no Jest that are Sharp Biting and if you Deliver any thing witty and Pleasant abstain from Laughing thereat yourself.

48. Wherein you reprove Another be unblameable yourself; for example is more prevalent than Precepts.

49. Use no Reproachful Language against any one neither Curse nor Revile.

50. Be not hasty to believe flying Reports to the Disparagement of any.

51. Wear not your Cloths, foul, ripped or Dusty but See they be Brushed once every day at least and take heed that you approach not to any Uncleanness.

52. In your Apparel be Modest and endeavour to accommodate Nature, rather than to procure Admiration keep to the Fashion of your equals Such as are Civil and orderly with respect to Times and Places.

53. Run not in the Streets, neither go too slowly nor with Mouth open go not Shaking your Arms, kick not the earth with your feet, go not upon the Toes, nor in a Dancing fashion.

54. Play not the Peacock, looking every where about you, to See if you be well Decked, if your Shoes fit well if your Stockings sit neatly, and Cloths handsomely.

55. Eat not in the Streets, nor in the House, out of Season.

56. Associate yourself with Men of good Quality if you Esteem your own Reputation; for 'tis better to be alone than in bad Company.

57. In walking up and Down in a House, only with One in Company if he be Greater than yourself, at the first give him the Right hand and Stop not till he does and be not the first that turns, and when you do turn let it be with your face towards him, if he be a Man of Great Quality, walk not with him Cheek by Jowl but Somewhat behind him; but yet in Such a Manner that he may easily Speak to you.

58. Let your Conversation be without Malice or Envy, for 'tis a Sign of a Tractable and Commendable Nature: And in all Causes of Passion admit Reason to Govern.

59. Never express anything unbecoming, nor Act against the Rules Moral before your inferiours.

60. Be not immodest in urging your Friends to Discover a Secret.

61. Utter not base and frivolous things amongst grave and Learned Men nor very Difficult Questions or Subjects, among the Ignorant or things hard to be believed, Stuff not your Discourse with Sentences amongst your Betters nor Equals.

62. Speak not of doleful Things in a Time of Mirth or at the Table; Speak not of Melancholy Things as Death and Wounds, and if others Mention them Change if you can the Discourse tell not your Dreams, but to your intimate Friend.

63. A Man ought not to value himself of his Achievements, or rare Qualities of wit; much less of his riches Virtue or Kindred.

64. Break not a Jest where none take pleasure in mirth Laugh not aloud, nor at all without Occasion, deride no mans Misfortune, though there Seem to be Some cause.

65. Speak not injurious Words neither in Jest nor Earnest Scoff at none although they give Occasion.

66. Be not forward but friendly and Courteous; the first to Salute hear and answer & be not Pensive when it's a time to Converse.

67. Detract not from others neither be excessive in Commanding.

68. Go not thither, where you know not, whether you Shall be Welcome or not. Give not Advice without being Asked & when desired do it briefly.

69. If two contend together take not the part of either unconstrained; and be not obstinate in your own Opinion, in Things indifferent be of the Major Side.

70. Reprehend not the imperfections of others for that belongs to Parents Masters and Superiours.

71. Gaze not on the marks or blemishes of Others and ask not how they came. What you may Speak in Secret to your Friend deliver not before others.

72. Speak not in an unknown Tongue in Company but in your own Language and that as those of Quality do and not as the Vulgar; Sublime matters treat Seriously.

73. Think before you Speak pronounce not imperfectly nor bring out your Words too hastily but orderly & distinctly.

74. When Another Speaks be attentive your Self and disturb not the Audience if any hesitate in his Words help him not nor Prompt him without desired, Interrupt him not, nor Answer him till his Speech be ended.

75. In the midst of Discourse ask not of what one treateth but if you Perceive any Stop because of [your coming you may well intreat him gently to Proceed: If a Person of Quality comes in while your Conversing it's handsome to Repeat what was said before.

76. While you are talking, Point not with your Finger at him of Whom you Discourse nor Approach too near him to whom you talk especially to his face.

77. Treat with men at fit Times about Business & Whisper not in the Company of Others.

78. Make no Comparisons and if any of the Company be Commended for any brave act of Virtue, commend not another for the Same.

79. Be not apt to relate News if you know not the truth thereof. In Discoursing of things you Have heard Name not your Author always A Secret Discover not.

80. Be not Tedious in Discourse or in reading unless you find the Company pleased therewith.

81. Be not Curious to Know the Affairs of Others neither approach those that Speak in Private.

82. Undertake not what you cannot Perform but be Careful to keep your Promise.

83. When you deliver a matter do it without Passion & with Discretion, however mean the Person be you do it too.

84. When your Superiours talk to any Body hearken not neither Speak nor Laugh.

85. In Company of these of Higher Quality than yourself Speak not til you are asked a Question then Stand upright put of your Hat & Answer in few words.

86. In Disputes, be not So Desirous to Overcome as not to give Liberty to each one to deliver his Opinion and Submit to the Judgment of the Major Part especially if they are Judges of the Dispute.

87. Let thy carriage be such as becomes a Man Grave Settled and attentive to that which is spoken. Contradict not at every turn what others Say.

88. Be not tedious in Discourse, make not many Digressions, nor repeat often the Same manner of Discourse.

89. Speak not Evil of the absent for it is unjust.

90. Being Set at meat Scratch not neither Spit Cough or blow your Nose except there's a Necessity for it.

91. Make no Show of taking great Delight in your Victuals, Feed not with Greediness; cut your Bread with a Knife, lean not on the Table neither find fault with what you Eat.

92. Take no Salt or cut Bread with your Knife Greasy.

93. Entertaining any one at table it is decent to present him with meat, Undertake not to help others undesired by the Master.

94. If you Soak bread in the Sauce let it be no more than what you put in your Mouth at a time and blow not your broth at Table but Stay till Cools of it Self.

95. Put not your meat to your Mouth with your Knife in your hand neither Spit forth the Stones of any fruit Pie upon a Dish nor Cast anything under the table.

96. It's unbecoming to Stoop much to ones Meat Keep your Fingers clean & when foul wipe them on a Corner of your Table Napkin.

97. Put not another bite into your Mouth til the former be Swallowed let not your Morsels be too big for the Jowls.

98. Drink not nor talk with your mouth full neither Gaze about you while you are a Drinking.

99. Drink not too leisurely nor yet too hastily. Before and after Drinking wipe your Lips breath not then or Ever with too Great a Noise, for its uncivil.

100. Cleanse not your teeth with the Table Cloth Napkin Fork or Knife but if Others do it let it be done wt. a Pick Tooth.

101. Rinse not your Mouth in the Presence of Others.

102. It is out of use to call upon the Company often to Eat nor need you Drink to others every Time you Drink.

103. In Company of your Betters be not longer in eating than they are lay not your Arm but only your hand upon the table.

104. It belongs to the Chiefest in Company to unfold his Napkin and fall to Meat first, But he ought then to Begin in time & to Dispatch with Dexterity that the Slowest may have time allowed him.

105. Be not Angry at Table whatever happens & if you have reason to be so, Show it not but on a Cheerful Countenance especially if there be Strangers for Good Humour makes one Dish of Meat a Feast.

106. Set not yourself at the upper of the Table but if it Be your Due or that the Master of the house will have it So, Contend not, least you Should Trouble the Company.

107. If others talk at Table be attentive but talk not with Meat in your Mouth.

108. When you Speak of God or his Attributes, let it be Seriously & with Reverence. Honour & Obey your Natural Parents although they be Poor.

109. Let your Recreations be Manful not Sinful.

110. Labour to keep alive in your Breast that Little Spark of Celestial fire Called Conscience.

# ADDITIONAL RESOURCES

"Test your Emotional Intelligence," free EQ Quiz by the Institute of Health and Human Potential. Access it at: https://www.ihhp.com/free-eq-quiz/

*Unique Ability: Creating the Life You Want*, by Catherine Nomura and Julia Waller, The Strategic Coach Inc., 1995

*Take The Reins! 7 Secrets to Inspired Leadership*, by Shari Jaeger Goodwin, Shari Jaeger Goodwin, 2013

*How Did That Happen? Holding People Accountable for Results The Positive, Principled Way*, by Roger Connors and Tom Smith, Penguin Group (USA) LLC, 2009

*Coaching Questions: A Coach's Guide to Powerful Asking Skills* by Tony Stoltzfus, Coach22 Bookstore LLC, 2008.

54119792R00065

Made in the USA
Columbia, SC
28 March 2019